# The Buffett Essays Symposium

## A 20th Anniversary Annotated Transcript

*with*

## Warren Buffett & Charlie Munger

*hosted and edited by*

## Lawrence A. Cunningham

# The Buffett Essays Symposium

A 20th Anniversary Annotated Transcript

*with*

Warren Buffett & Charlie Munger

*hosted and edited by*

Lawrence A. Cunningham

Published and Distributed as a Joint Venture by

**The Cunningham Group**

&

**Harriman House**

Copyright © 2016 Lawrence A. Cunningham

Library of Congress Cataloging-in-Publication Data
Cunningham, Lawrence A., 1962-
The Buffett Essays Symposium / Lawrence Cunningham.
pages cm
Includes transcription of live dialogue and annotation.

Paperback ISBN: 978-0-85719-538-8

eBook ISBN: 978-0-85719-539-5

1. Berkshire Hathaway Inc. 2. Buffett, Warren.
3. Munger, Charlie. 4. Investments. 5. Management

*No one has a monopoly on truth or wisdom.*
*We make progress by listening to each other.*

ELENA KAGAN

*A conversation is a dialogue, not a monologue.*

TRUMAN CAPOTE

*Tell me and I forget. Teach me and I remember.*
*Involve me and I learn.*

BENJAMIN FRANKLIN

# Contents

Prologue ix

Production Note xxi

Contributors xxv

Greetings from Dean David Rudenstine 1

Corporate Governance 3

Finance and Investing 23

Mergers and Acquisitions 41

Accounting and Taxation 57

Reminiscences 79

Gallery 83

Subsequent Steps 87

Notes from Omaha 96

Epilogue 97

Index 101

# Prologue

I NTELLECTUAL SPARKS FLEW AMONG WARREN BUFFETT, Charlie Munger, and other guests at the 1996 symposium to launch *The Essays of Warren Buffett: Lessons for Corporate America*—then a manuscript few guessed would become an international bestseller. After governance expert Ira Millstein declared that boards must develop strategic plans for acquisitions, Buffett countered that "more dumb acquisitions are done in the name of strategic plans than any other." When I and a colleague acknowledged including modern finance theory in our teaching, Munger chastised us for peddling "twaddle and gibberish"—quickly adding, "I like both these guys."

The two-day conference in New York City began on a Sunday in October, the day after the New York Yankees won the World Series. We probed profound issues of corporate life, topics still being argued about today by shareholders, directors, executives, judges, and scholars. I recently came upon the original tapes of the conference after an old friend, Peter Bevelin, asked me about the event. I had not examined this material in two decades but, when I did, I was struck by how many of the questions we discussed remain vital today. *Plus ça change, plus c'est la même chose.*

For Buffett, change and continuity have been dominant themes since 1956. Back then, the 26-year-old prodigy formed a partnership to acquire small businesses and equity stakes in larger companies. In 1965, the partnership took control of Berkshire Hathaway Inc., a publicly-held and struggling textile manufacturer. The Buffett Partnership soon dissolved, with Berkshire shares distributed to the partners, Munger chief among them. Berkshire proceeded to acquire interests in diverse businesses, including insurance, manufacturing, and retailing.

Under Buffett and Munger, Berkshire has gone through two massive transformations. In the first, the company went from a failed textile manufacturer into a prosperous investment vehicle by 1996. At that time, assets were comprised of 80% marketable securities and 20% in operating companies. In the second, since 1996, Berkshire morphed into a massive conglomerate. Today its assets are comprised 80% of operating companies and 20% marketable securities, though the latter's market value exceeds $100 billion.

Performance has been stellar: through 2015, results vastly exceeded benchmarks such as the Dow Jones Industrial Average or Standard & Poor's 500. From 1965 to 2015, the Dow increased 18-fold while Berkshire increased 12,000 times, a compound annual rate of 21%, double the S&P.

Despite changing from the partnership to the corporate form, Buffett preserved Berkshire's sense of partnership. The legacy is reflected in the first of 15 principles stated for decades in Berkshire's "owners' manual": "While our form is corporate, our attitude is partnership." The "Berkshire system," as Munger dubbed it in 2015, differs significantly from prevailing practices at other large American corporations.

Buffett provides unconventional takes on numerous topics of corporate life, which is why his company and writings have been so fascinating to study all these years. In governance, the Berkshire emphasis is on trust not control; on mergers, Buffett favors letting shareholders rather than boards make final decisions; in corporate finance, he shuns debt and attracted legions of followers to the field of value investing; and on accounting and taxation, he shaped debates from stock options to merger accounting and raised public attention to inequality in his famous declaration that his secretary's tax rate exceeds his own.

Buffett's writings are primarily contained in his letters to Berkshire shareholders, the centerpiece of the symposium. After carefully reviewing all those letters, I rearranged and collated them by topic into a 150-page booklet for the symposium: governance, investing, acquisitions, accounting, and taxation. At the symposium, a series of panels examined each, spanning more than twelve hours.

Soon after, I prepared an edited version of the formal remarks and supervised the publication of a resulting academic volume of 800 pages, consisting of 18 articles and a transcript of 100 pages. In the two decades since, several of the articles have become classics in their fields and I have regularly released updated editions of *The Essays of Warren Buffett: Lessons for Corporate America*, which has been translated into a dozen languages.

I invited Warren to participate in the symposium and volunteered to rearrange and republish his letters because my research indicated that they were valuable but underappreciated. I was honored that he accepted. He spent two days with a great crowd, which included many of my students, along with a dozen business law professors whom I enlisted to speak on the panels. Among these was my own teacher, Elliott Weiss, who first introduced me to Buffett's writings and worked closely with Warren a decade earlier on a national project to improve disclosure in corporate America.

The symposium also brought together many distinguished people from Berkshire's orbit, including Warren's wife Susan and son Howard; their friend and editor of Warren's annual letters, Carol Loomis; their friend and later Berkshire director Sandy Gottesman and his wife Ruth, a professor at Albert Einstein College of Medicine; Warren's personal attorney George Gillespie and Berkshire attorney Bob Denham; Berkshire executives Ajit Jain and Lou Simpson; and long-time Berkshire shareholder and devotee, Chris Stavrou. Two panels were led by other notable figures: long-time Berkshire shareholder Louis Lowenstein, former president of Supermarkets General Corporation and professor at Columbia University (also the father of Buffett biographer, Roger Lowenstein), and Ira Millstein, a distinguished attorney and leader of the National Association of Corporate Directors.

Among many other notables in the audience of 150 were Bill Ackman, Bruce Berkowitz, and Paul Hilal, all to become prominent investors; Otis Bilodeau, then a student of mine at George Washington University and today the global executive editor of Bloomberg Television; The Honorable Jack Jacobs, then of the Delaware Chancery Court and later a Justice on the Delaware Supreme Court; Marjorie Knowles, an official at TIAA-CREF; and Bob Mundheim, among those who Buffett hand-selected to manage Salomon Brothers after he became its reluctant interim chairman in 1991 following a bond trading scandal at the Wall Street investment bank.

Our discussion was vibrant, so provided below are a few highlights on each panel to give a taste and provide context for what follows in this volume. You might also consider skimming the index to locate topics of special interest. Of particular note are the entries under "Buffett quips," "Buffett tutorials," "Munger quips," and "Munger tutorials."

# Corporate Governance

Traditionally, CEOs of public companies wielded considerable power and the board tended to reinforce rather than check that power. In the late 1970s, the model began to shift after the Foreign Corrupt Practices Act of 1977 asked for more oversight from boards and in the 1990s once the Federal Organizational Sentencing Guidelines of 1991 gave corporations credit for adopting formal oversight programs.

By the time of our symposium in 1996, such regulations forced boards to assume a new role, one focused on monitoring. That meant independent directors, often a powerful non-executive chairman or lead director, along with numerous strong committees, all overseeing elaborate systems of internal control. Since 1996, the monitoring model has become mandatory for public corporations, through laws such as the Sarbanes-Oxley Act of 2002 and the Dodd-Frank Act of 2010.

With few exceptions, such reforms applied equally to all public companies without regard to specific features, such as ownership demographics, corporate cultures, management structures, or other governance design features. They ignored a typology of governance that Buffett famously identified which, he believes, require different board roles: (1) those with a controlling shareholder who is also the manager, which has been Berkshire's model; (2) those with a controlling shareholder who is not a manager, which will characterize Berkshire after Buffett leaves the scene; and (3) those without a controlling shareholder, which will ultimately be Berkshire's position in the decades after Buffett's estate distributes all his shares.

Berkshire has always had an advisory board, not a monitoring one, even after all the reforms and regulations that swept across corporate America from 1977 to 2010. After all, Buffett's controlling position has allowed him to nominate and elect Berkshire's board of directors from the outset. During that time, Berkshire's board came to assume characteristics quite different from that of typical public companies today. From the earliest decades, the board included Buffett's wife and close friends and, since 1993, his son. A classic advisory board, members met infrequently and exercised few oversight functions.

*Warren Buffett at the symposium*

Today, Berkshire's board adheres to legal requirements concerning requisite committees, independence, and expertise. But these devices and labels appear to be form over substance. For one, all directors have close personal and professional relationships with Buffett and are handpicked by him. Examples: primary beneficiary of Buffett's will Bill Gates (via the Bill and Melinda Gates Foundation); long-time friend, Sandy Gottesman; and chief Berkshire outside counsel, Ron Olson. In addition, half the board members are older than sixty-five and most have served Berkshire for a decade or more—facts that would compel their departure under typical age-limit and term-limit regimes endorsed by governance gurus.

Berkshire's principal parent-level activity is accumulating and allocating capital, often making substantial acquisitions. At most companies, CEOs might formulate a general acquisition program and then present specific proposals to the board for approval. As Ira Millstein noted at the symposium, most boards adopt strategic plans and oversee their implementation; as Buffett responded, Berkshire has never had one. The absence of a plan, however, enables Buffett to seize opportunities for Berkshire that would be lost if prior board involvement were required.

Buffett shares with the board the general philosophy of acquisitions and might discuss large deals with it in advance in conceptual terms. But the board is uninvolved in valuation, structuring, or funding any specific acquisition. With few exceptions, the board does not find out about an acquisition until after it is publicly announced. Rather, overtures, discussions, and negotiations are kept confidential, limited at most to a few Berkshire insiders, typically including Munger.

Berkshire's board has two regularly scheduled board meetings annually, not the typical eight to twelve at other Fortune 500 companies. Before each meeting, directors receive a report from Berkshire's internal auditing team. Berkshire's spring board meeting coincides with Berkshire's annual shareholders' meeting in May. Directors spend several days in Omaha, corporate headquarters, mingling in social gatherings with Berkshire officers, subsidiary managers, and shareholders. The fall meeting features opportunities to meet one or more CEOs of Berkshire subsidiaries, either in Omaha or at a sub's corporate headquarters. One or more CEOs make presentations and exchange ideas with the directors and fellow unit chiefs.

According to director Susan Decker, Berkshire's approach to board meetings, especially involving the directors in Berkshire events outside of the boardroom, produces a "strong inculcation of culture." Cynics might say such an environment promotes structural bias that can impair the independent judgment corporate governance advocates have hailed in recent decades. And it is not flawless—the vast power Buffett wields has led to several nontrivial acquisition mistakes, though the net gains from his leadership have been overwhelming. Moreover, the immersion of directors in Berkshire culture flattens the typical hierarchies of corporate governance, keeping directors in shareholders' shoes; their optimal vantage point, whatever the governance gurus might prescribe.

*Charlie Munger (gesturing) and Howard Buffett
at the symposium*

# Finance and Investing

While Buffett has been heralded as a "relational" investor, participants at the symposium spent some time discussing what that concept means. Buffett never called himself a relational investor and does not believe in the concept. The concept, moreover, while fashionable in the 1990s, has been eclipsed by the broader and more powerful category of shareholder activism.

On the other hand, Berkshire and its shareholders all seem to be engaged in a genuine relational investment association, hailed by the partnership conception Buffett minted and repeats. At the symposium, a commentator observed that Buffett's repeated assertions that Berkshire was a partnership among him and all shareholders could well be legally binding and Buffett would owe fellow owners fiduciary duties of loyalty far more stringent than those corporate directors owe shareholders. Buffett said that would be fine with him. So while Berkshire may not exemplify what most people meant by relational investing, its model is even more profound, showing that long-term gain is compatible with fidelity to fellow shareholders.

The mid-1990s were also an inflection point for modern finance theory, which portrays stock markets as efficient and price activity as the basic measure of risk. The model swept not only the academy but many in the investing and corporate worlds. Yet it denied the possibility of any given investor systematically outperforming the stock market, as its numerous participants rapidly digest information to drive prices to the best estimates of value. That made Buffett an anomaly, with devotees of modern finance theory dismissing him as merely lucky. At the symposium, discussion generally treated modern finance theory skeptically, with a few impassioned opponents too, epitomized by Munger's disdainful characterizations of it as "gibberish" and "twaddle."

Not only do Buffett and Berkshire depart from conventional wisdom, Berkshire's other shareholders are also a different breed. Typically, large public companies see seventy to eighty percent of their shares controlled by institutional investors. Decisions are often by committee and based on financial models that can lead to trading the stock for reasons unrelated to the company. In contrast, most Berkshire shares are owned by individuals and families who make investment decisions based on Berkshire's specific characteristics.

Berkshire shareholders have unusually long holding periods. In the past decade, share turnover has been less than one percent compared to three, four, or five percent for other conglomerates, large insurance companies, or Berkshire's formerly-public subsidiaries. At the symposium, when Berkshire's shares were trading for $30,000 per share, Buffett stated that ninety percent of the shares had a basis of less than $100—meaning that they had been held for two or three decades.

Berkshire's dividend policy was addressed at the symposium. Aside from a small dividend in 1969, it has never paid one. Buffett repeatedly explains Berkshire's policy, which is to retain each dollar of earnings so long as it translated into at least one dollar of market value. Berkshire polled its shareholders on this policy in 1984—and again in 2014—with a uniform answer: they overwhelmingly endorsed the policy, more than ninety percent affirming. In 1996, after Berkshire stock traded at $30,000, some shareholders needing cash or wishing to make gifts, signaled interest in lower-priced shares. At this time, as Berkshire's stellar performance became well known, demand rose among non-shareholders for a more affordable piece of the action.

In 1996, inspired by demand, two financiers designed an investment vehicle to meet it. They proposed to create unit trusts that would buy the expensive Berkshire shares and then issue fractional interests at far lower trading prices of around $500 each. To eliminate the appeal of such trusts, and associated fees the promoters planned to charge, Berkshire created two classes of stock, one with fractional voting and economic rights, set to trade at around $1,000 per share. The move, aptly called "ingenious" at the symposium, also enabled existing Berkshire shareholders to create liquidity, as the pricey Class A shares can be converted, tax-free, into the cheaper Class B shares.

# Mergers and Acquisitions

Through 1996, Berkshire had made only a handful of important acquisitions. Buffett's involvement in mergers had concerned companies—such as Gillette and Salomon Brothers—in which Berkshire owned stock or where Buffett was a director. From that vantage point, their central concern was making sure boards did not interfere with shareholder opportunity for obtaining the best value for their shares.

Persistent fundamental questions are whether bidders overpay with takeover premiums or pick up targets on the cheap and the role corporate culture might play in a board's response to an unwanted overture. Above all, the enduring question is if takeover artists then and shareholder activists today add or subtract value? Are they con artists, fools or visionaries?

In the intervening two decades, Buffett gradually resigned his board posts and Berkshire's investments increasingly are for 100% of companies through merger or acquisition rather than minority stakes. Since 1996, Berkshire has become a major acquirer of companies, laying out approximately $170 billion in about 40 acquisitions, dwarfing the dozen much smaller acquisitions made before that. So while Buffett's positions on these perennial topics remain the same—favoring shareholder choice, expecting gaps between price versus value, believing in corporate culture, and disfavoring hostile bids and public activism—Berkshire's role differs greatly.

Specifically, Buffett built a conglomerate, the kind of company that takeover artists as of 1996 had been busting up and that shareholder activists since have been trying to trim. In the earlier era, Kohlberg Kravis Roberts (KKR) waged campaigns to dismantle conglomerates in much the way that Carl Icahn and Nelson Peltz do today. But in both eras, Buffett and Berkshire embraced the conglomerate model—acquiring the conglomerate Scott Fetzer in a white knight transaction in 1986 and by 2006 establishing Berkshire as the great American corporate colossus.

True to perceptions in 1996, Buffett has cemented a distinctive trust-based corporate culture at Berkshire in the two decades since. At most companies, especially conglomerates, corporate tasks tend to be centralized, with divisional and sub-division heads ("middle management"), reporting hierarchies, systematic policies concerning budgeting, personnel, and intricate systems of procedures. Such structures require incremental costs in the name of effective oversight.

In contrast, with the exception of a basic internal auditing function, Berkshire eschews such staples of corporate life as bureaucratic excess. Berkshire devolves these and all other internal matters to its subsidiaries. Home office overhead is negligible at Berkshire, with a staff of only two dozen, focused primarily on financial reporting and auditing. Each subsidiary maintains its own programs and policies concerning budgeting, operations, and personnel—as well as conventional departments such as accounting, compliance, human resources, legal, marketing, technology, and so on.

Berkshire only acquires companies with strong top management in place and then defers to them with scant supervision. All quotidian decisions qualify: advertising budget; product features and environmental quality; the product mix and pricing. The same applies to decisions about hiring, merchandising, inventory, and receivables management.

Berkshire's deference extends to subsidiary decisions on succession to senior positions, including chief executive officer. Berkshire rarely transfers businesses between subsidiaries and hardly ever moves managers around. Berkshire has no retirement policy and many chief executives work into their seventies or eighties. Berkshire culture is designed as a permanent home for an eclectic mix of autonomous, self-reliant and thrifty, prosperous businesses.

*Larry Cunningham and Charlie Munger during a break*

# Accounting and Taxation

Buffett is noted for his lucid accounting explanations in his annual reports, which often include alternative presentations and explanations not required or contemplated by formal accounting rules or securities laws. At the symposium, the habit prompted debate about whether shareholders are better served by disclosure that solely adheres to requirements or ventures the broader views of top managers. In 1996, the context highlighted contemporary alternatives of accounting for mergers—pooling or purchase—but the broader topic remains lively as rules were changed to regulate non-GAAP disclosures in stringent ways, even as investors demand supplemental non-GAAP information.

While Buffett drew attention to income inequality in a 2011 *New York Times* op-ed by the dramatic statement that his secretary paid a higher tax rate than he, Munger emphatically made the same case for income tax fairness at the symposium in 1996. Fairness and rationality are fixtures in tax policy debate, whether the income tax itself or the many contentious issues of corporate taxation. At the symposium, topics spanned from basics such as the relative rates applied to individuals versus corporations as well as tax incentives that influence corporate dividend policy, and the form and amount of executive compensation.

Tax policy debates raise perennial questions about the ethics of corporate tax minimization or avoidance. For instance, Berkshire's conglomerate structure enables internal cash reallocation to businesses generating the highest returns on incremental capital—without incurring income tax. Some subsidiaries generate tax credits in their businesses that they cannot use but which can be used by sister subsidiaries. Berkshire has financed corporate inversions, such as when the American icon Burger King reincorporated in Canada upon merging with Tim Hortons. Such were the timeless topics of our symposium and to which our transcript contributes ongoing value.

\* \* \* \* \*

The substance of the symposium's discussion resembled that addressed annually at Berkshire annual shareholders' meetings, though the format differed greatly. I first attended Berkshire's meeting in 1997, the spring after the symposium, which drew a record crowd of 7,500—what Warren warned me would be a "mob scene." Two decades later, I attended the 2015 meeting, which drew some 40,000. (We limited attendance at the symposium to 150.)

At the meetings, the main event is un-rehearsed and un-choreographed business discussion, where Buffett and Munger spend the day answering scores of questions from shareholders while sipping Coca-Cola and eating See's peanut brittle. At the symposium, the two Berkshire executives spent more time asking questions than answering them, and there was far more give-and-take colloquy. But we also served Coke and See's.

Lawrence A. Cunningham
New York, New York
Spring 2016

# Production Note

Along with the context provided by the Prologue, the edited transcript is annotated with current commentary by a host of special guests. These include leading investors and experts on Berkshire and Buffett, many of whom also attended the symposium, including Deborah DeMott, Robert Hagstrom, Paul Hilal, Mark Hughes, Ed Kitch, Dale Oesterle, Shane Parrish, and Jim Repetti.

While most of the humorous commentary translated well from videotape to print, the transcript nevertheless indicates the presence of laughter when the audience collectively chuckled. And while the videotapes and corresponding transcript captured the lion's share of the colloquy, there were a few gaps in some of the tapes.

On a style note, as with the original transcript, this one omits material without indicating omissions with ellipses or other punctuation; deletions include both lengthy statements that span paragraphs as well as utterances unworthy of print, such as verbal ticks, halting or redundant expression, and glue words.

Most photographs reprinted here are from the symposium and, other than those provided by the editor and other guests, all are courtesy of the communications office of Benjamin N. Cardozo School of Law, Yeshiva University, New York, where the symposium was held, specifically The Samuel and Ronnie Heyman Center on Corporate Governance, which I directed at the time.

Finally, thanks to those friends and colleagues who reviewed and commented on this annotated transcript, including the contributors listed above as well as Bill Ackman, Peter Bevelin, Jeff Gordon, Sandy Gottesman, Steve Keating, and Andy Kilpatrick. I'm especially grateful for the continued support and kind words about this transcript from Warren Buffett. Above all, thanks to my wife Stephanie Cuba, for everything under the sun, especially our daughters, Rebecca and Sarah.

L.A.C.

*Warren Buffett, Susan Buffett, George Gillespie*

*Sandy Gottesman, Ajit Jain, Carol Loomis*

*Larry Cunningham, Warren Buffett, David Rudenstine*

*Carol Loomis, Warren Buffett, Howard Buffett,*
*Sandy Gottesman, Ajit Jain*

*Susan Buffett, Warren Buffett,*
*Charlie Munger, Howard Buffett*

# Contributors

Ackman, William (Activist Investor, Pershing Square Capital)

Bratton, William W. (Professor, University of Pennsylvania)

Buffett, Warren E. (Berkshire Hathaway Inc.)

Cunningham, Lawrence A. (Professor, George Washington University)

Denham, Robert E. (Partner, Munger Tolles & Olson)

DeMott, Deborah A. (Professor, Duke University)

Eisenberg, Melvin A. (Professor, University of California at Berkeley)

Fisch, Jill E. (Professor, University of Pennsylvania)

Gordon, Jeffrey N. (Professor, Columbia University)

Hagstrom, Robert (Investor and Author)

Hamilton, Robert H. (Professor, University of Texas)

Hilal, Paul (Activist Investor, formerly Pershing Square Capital)

Holdcroft, James P., Jr. (Bank Executive)

Johnson, Calvin H. (Professor, University of Texas)

Kitch, Edmund A. (Professor, University of Virginia)

Klein, William (Professor Emeritus, UCLA)

Knowles, Marjorie (TIAA-CREF; Georgia State University)

Lowenstein, Louis (late Professor, Columbia University)

Macey, Jonathan R. (Professor, Yale University)

Millstein, Ira M. (Partner, Weil, Gotshal & Manges LLP)

Mundheim, Robert (Partner, Sherman & Sterling)

Munger, Charles T. (Berkshire Hathaway Inc.)

Oesterle, Dale Arthur (Professor, Ohio State University)

Reed, J. Bradbury (late Partner, Bass, Berry & Sims)

Repetti, James R. (Professor, Boston College)

Rudenstine, David (Former Dean, Cardozo School of Law)

Simpson, Louis (Retired Executive, GEICO)

Stout, Lynn A. (Professor, Cornell University)

Weiss, Elliott J. (Professor, University of Arizona)

Yablon, Charles M. (Professor, Cardozo School of Law)

---

*Current or recent affiliation given.*

# GREETINGS FROM DEAN DAVID RUDENSTINE

## October 27, 1996

WELCOME EVERYONE TO CARDOZO LAW SCHOOL. This is Cardozo's twentieth anniversary year, not long in the history of houses of learning, if you compare it to Harvard or Yale or Oxford or New York Institute of Fashion. But while we're still wet behind our ears, our story is remarkable, for in hardly any time, Cardozo has established itself as an important center of learning, scholarship, and teaching. Today's symposium is both the latest expression of this growing standing as well as a builder of it.

It hardly seems right to dive into *The Essays of Warren Buffett*, however, without first mentioning the Yankees' victory last night. After all, Buffett and the Yankees have in common at least their respective dominance in their fields. And last night the Yankees won the World Series for the first time in eighteen years. When I was growing up, they won all the time. I don't remember the 1947 championship because I was only five. But by 1949, I was in high gear and lived and died with the pitches and hits as the Yankees rolled through the glory years of the early fifties.

1

As you all know, Casey Stengel was the Yankee manager during those triumphant seasons. Like Warren Buffett, he attracted attention because, like Mr. Buffett, he was a winner. At the end of the day, month or year, you would check the standings and his Yankees would be on top. Unlike Mr. Buffett, however, Mr. Stengel did not write essays, did not write to the Yankees' owners, players, or fans. Yet he had plenty to say and as a prelude to spending two days thinking about what Mr. Buffett has written over the past many years, I thought I might quote some of Mr. Stengel's most astonishing remarks.

In a vein that might have captured last night's game, Stengel once said "Good pitching will always stop good hitting and vice versa." On whether abstinence from drinking helped players play better baseball, Stengel said "It only helps if they can play." On being decisive, the way you have to be as an investor, Stengel said "I made up my mind, but I made it up both ways." On his good fortune as a successful manager— and perhaps a comment that Mr. Buffett might feel resonance with— Stengel said "You make your own luck; some people have bad luck all their lives." And, lastly, on his future, Stengel said, in the spring of 1965, "How the hell should I know, most people my age are dead."

Conferences don't just happen. They take a creative mind, a strategic hand, hundreds of hours of organizing work and financial resources. Today's symposium is no exception. Professor Larry Cunningham conceived of this conference, shaped it, and organized it. We all owe Larry a huge debt, and thank you, Larry. We also want to thank the students of the Cardozo Law Review for helping Larry carry off his ambitious idea for this symposium. They worked diligently and we would not be here without their efforts—so thanks. Financial support for this symposium comes from the Samuel and Ronnie Heyman Center on Corporate Governance. The Heymans have been generous supporters of the Law School for many years. We are greatly indebted to them for their continuing support and faith in our capacity to do the kinds of things we are doing here today.

And lastly, I want to thank Warren Buffett for his essays and for his presence. We all very much appreciate your participation and eagerly look forward to the next two days of discussion.

# CORPORATE GOVERNANCE

*Panel One: Chaired by Ira Millstein (at right, back to camera)*
*Front Row: Susan Buffett, Warren Buffett, Charlie Munger*
*Second Row: Bruce Berkowitz, Peter Hilal, Bill Ackman, Paul Hilal*

\* \* \* \* \*

*Jonathan Macey and James Holdcroft proposed a radical idea: to let shareholders of a public company annually vote by proxy in favor of directing the board either to replace incumbent management or put the company up for sale.*

BOB DENHAM: This proposal seems to me a particularly interesting example of what I see as a dangerous strain in corporate governance reform proposals. It's a strain that we see in corporate governance reform by separating power from responsibility. And this proposal could involve a particularly radical separation of power from responsibility. The shareholders would have the power to hang a "for sale" sign on the company but would not have the responsibility to carry that out.

And, of course, in many situations it's not the best way to sell a company to put a for sale sign on it. That can destabilize employees and customers and it may not be a good prospect for selling a company under the circumstances that led shareholders to put that for sale sign on. By separating power from responsibility in this way, I have trouble imagining why any sane person would serve on a board.

HOLDCROFT: We think actually the contrary here—that this brings responsibility in line with the decision making. The shareholders are going to be the ones who will have the gain or loss based on the actions of the directors either way. So this is allowing them to make the decisions when they think it's appropriate.

BOB MUNDHEIM: I was going to ask the same kind of question that Bob Denham did. For example, assume the shareholders of a brokerage firm hung up a for sale sign. What happens to the people inside during the period while they're trying to sell it?

MACEY: Some companies are going to be better to sell than others, and it would be perfectly reasonable annually for the directors, when they're sending out this solicitation which would have the voting options that we're envisioning to say: we recommend you don't sell the company, and it would have these terrible consequences.

And if your analysis is right, then you have this brokerage firm and there would be this nightmarish problem and all these people would be leaving during the period of the sale, that this firm would lose a lot of value if it were sold in this very bad way. And all I'm saying is if that's true, it's going to be the decision makers here—the shareholders—who bear that cost.

MUNDHEIM: The directors might not be able to make that statement if, in fact, during that period, they are trying to sell the company. I don't know that in the proxy statement, consistent with securities laws, they can say it would be a dreadful thing to sell it and then shortly thereafter announce the sale (laughter).

MACEY: That's right, and you have a similar point if you have some really great piece of information that a company has and you force the sale of a company. But we would certainly in our proposal give the board of directors significant leeway with respect to timing so that even if they got this vote, and the kind of special facts you're describing—like they're already trying to sell the company or there's some piece of corporate information that's not public that would have a radical change on the price and you couldn't let that out at an auction—those are really easy changes.

PAUL HILAL: We sell companies on a daily basis, and we go to great lengths, always to make sure that the offer process is kept confidential. Because even the possibility that my client would be up for sale is a terror not only for the employees—causing defections and the circulation of resumes—but also suppliers and customers. So, one would argue that even the potential that each year the entire company can be put up for sale or the senior management structure could be swept out would in and of itself compromise the corporation or prevent it from achieving full value.

The proposal that you laid out juxtaposes an alternative for this shareholder-first regime. Right now the shareholders of a widely held corporation have little direct influence, but they have the alternative of selling their shares and walking from a management team they don't support.

Your proposal would give the dispersed shareholder greater direct influence and control, inviting the question: does the shareholder know enough to be so empowered? Aren't you pointing to a failure of the representative system that depends upon election of savvy, deeply engaged board members? Isn't the point here simply that those board members sometimes fail to represent the interests of their constituents? So perhaps a better remedy would be at the board level, rather than increasing the direct influence of shareholders who may or may not be best positioned to exercise that influence?

MACEY: I think it's important to think for just a second about the fact that every year companies are sending out proxy solicitations, every year shareholders are voting, and we have a very strong empirical record that shows overwhelmingly that management is winning these proxy contests. They control the proxy machinery and we're even having corporate disruptions of the kind you and Dean Mundheim suggest. You're going to get exactly what we observed today, which is companies aren't going to be sold. And our proposal is directed at what we regard as the rare case.

IRA MILLSTEIN: Warren, I think the point they're making is a good one in a sense. If you were the sole shareholder or major shareholder of one of these companies and you wanted to change management, you could change it, or if you wanted to sell the company, you'd sell it. And what they're trying to do is find a way to get this dispersed ownership to be able to do what you can do as the sole owner. The real issue is whether you can translate sole ownership into dispersed ownership and get activity. Do you have a view on that?

BUFFETT: Well, at Berkshire we are the sole shareholder of our subsidiaries. In effect, we act as you would hope a board of directors would act representing dispersed shareholders. We just have a couple of problems. We have a capital allocation problem where the managers of the businesses would probably allocate capital differently than we would at Berkshire, because we don't care about the relative size of the subsidiaries. We care about the relative profitability of the shareholders of that subsidiary in effect in aggregate.

We also have the problem of dealing with whether we have the right managers and most of the time we do. The biggest problem is not the terrible manager. The biggest problem is the mediocre manager—and that's true everywhere. That is a very difficult thing to deal with, and I'm not sure how you deal with it. At Berkshire we can deal with it, but I would say it's my most difficult problem.

MILLSTEIN: For dispersed owners it must be even more of a difficult problem—how do you find that mediocre manager who is often very well hidden in the first place?

BUFFETT: It is very easy to do if you're running an athletic team. But our problems are really very similar. I would say that the biggest factor causing boards to act as they would act in our situation where we own 100% is embarrassment. If you embarrass big shots, they will behave better. And in that respect, probably the press has done more to cause boards to behave as they should than anything we can dream up.

\* \* \* \* \*

*Melvin Eisenberg argued that boards should maintain internal controls to assure corporate compliance with law and company policy. Jill Fisch argued that prevailing corporate governance talk favors a one-size fits all system ill-suited to the variety of firm-specific characteristics—citing Berkshire as a company better off by defying governance trends.*

*Marjorie Knowles*

MARJORIE KNOWLES: I would like to comment on two sides of this. First, it's not clear from Macey and Holdcroft what the proposal is supposed to cure. Was it supposed to cure the fact that takeovers take too long or to address the fact that most institutional investors are very conservative? I understand if you think it would go faster if shareholders could vote on whether to put the company up for sale, but the second problem seems to remain.

It is always a problem to lump shareholders together because they are so varied in both their purposes and processes. I can tell you from TIAA-CREF's experience that in terms of identifying underperforming companies and then doing something about them, the situation is much more complex than the press often makes it seem. We have found it not easy to identify underperforming companies in a way that is useful to us to take corporate governance action, and I don't think that's for the reasons you mentioned, Professor Fisch.

Let me explain it a little bit more. One of the themes that I always tell my students is the chorus from a Statler Brothers' song: "Life gets complicated when you get past eighteen." (Laughter.) I think the situation with institutional investors identifying underperforming companies and then doing something useful about it is an important subject. I don't think just putting these things on the proxy statement is a way that is most useful.

It's much more useful to distinguish among types of institutional investors. For example, corporate pension funds are notoriously conservative—that is, non-activist. Public pension funds may be more activist but less on the performance side than on the governance side. We tend to focus on the performance side, and we have found that there are a range of informal routes to deal with, none of which have to do with putting these things to shareholder votes.

My second point, I would like to respond to what you said, Professor Fisch, about not finding a correlation between corporate governance monitoring and performance. I'm not sure that's what we should be looking for, although I think the empirical evidence and the anecdotal evidence is that good corporate governance is most important for companies in times of transition or crisis. And I haven't seen good studies that measure that. Jay Lorsch's studies of how boards actually work show that governance norms come into play most when companies need a new succession plan, for example.

So I would say that by focusing on corporate governance norms, we intend to help companies plan better for times of crisis rather than increase the stock price over five years, which is what most business school studies study. [At TIAA-CREF], we are long-term investors and we are much more concerned about the long-term improvements in corporate performance rather than the short-term measurements that I've seen in the studies.

MILLSTEIN: We're trying to compare two models. One is a Buffett model of significant ownership and really paying attention to what's happening with management, and the TIAA-CREF model which is the epitome of the large public institution—which owns 1600 companies and really can't pay attention to all of them. It's impossible, but that is the way the world is going. When you track through the twenty-five largest companies, you find virtually the same twenty-five institutions owning virtually the same twenty-five companies. Now, as an antitrust lawyer that gives me great concern, but I seem to be the only one in the room with that concern! However, that's a fact of life. How does TIAA-CREF begin to identify Warren Buffett-type concerns amongst its 1600 companies?

KNOWLES: I'm glad to have an opportunity to explain about this company, which I admire a lot, but you're absolutely right. The overwhelming majority of our stock portfolio is passively invested or indexed. A comparatively small proportion is actively managed, and if we want to find out more about companies we would ask our analyst. We have found, and the Robert Pozen studies show, that it may not pay for most large institutional investors to put a lot of time and research into finding problems that they then go about fixing.

We have found, however, that with a couple of "under-performing companies," to the extent they can be located and measured effectively, working with management is our best way to go. And not just then, but for the life of the company. In fact, in our experience most under-performing managements have some story and the question is whether our analysts think their story is a good one and therefore that we should stick with them. We're too big to go around selling very often and that's our real problem. We have used the withholding of votes when we think a board of directors is being really irresponsible. Then comes the hard question: since we tend to be a large, public, but quiet company, do we hold a press conference or not: And I think that goes back to the point Mr. Buffett has raised.

MILLSTEIN: When it really gets bad you put the flashlight on, right? Mel?

EISENBERG: I don't want to rain on the tea party but you said you agreed with Jill. I don't think you did and I don't agree with you (laughter). Because you said that you agreed that every corporation should be able to have its own board structure, but I thought I heard Jill saying that a corporation should be able to decide it doesn't want an independent board. [Jill Fisch nodded.] And according to the summary you gave us of the new NACD report, one thing a company should do is to have an independent board.

MILLSTEIN: Absolutely.

EISENBERG: Okay, so I just want to make clear that we don't have as much harmony as has been rumored, number one. I also don't agree with you in that—or the report, I should say—when it says that the board should do anything it wants (beyond independence, I guess). Because, for example, as you could tell from my earlier presentation, I would be rather shocked if a board said we wash our hands of internal controls. At this corporation, we decide we're not interested in internal controls. I don't see it. I would be surprised if a board said, at this corporation we don't approve major corporate plans and actions. Uh-uh. Anything the corporation—executives—want, we rubber stamp. So, either you really don't mean what you say—you have of course two weeks to change it (laughter)—but either you really don't mean what you say or I disagree with it pretty profoundly.

MILLSTEIN: No, I mean what I say. I wouldn't think for a minute that a reasonably intelligent board would do any of the things you suggest. We have twenty-three pages of suggestions in the report, and we say that if you reject them you ought to tell the shareholders why. So, in my view, if a board were to reject doing the kind of auditing you want and tell its shareholders why they were no longer going to audit, they would be removed relatively rapidly. We think sunlight and an explanation of why the board is doing what it is doing is the best way to get at it. And I agree with Warren that no reasonably intelligent board which is diligent and knows what its function is, is going to reject doing the things you suggest—I have a lot more confidence in these people than I guess you do. I think they'll do the right thing.

EISENBERG: Who is you?

MILLSTEIN: You.

EISENBERG: Me?

MILLSTEIN: Y-O-U, yes. You want to regulate them and tell them what to do?

EISENBERG: In some critical aspects I would say yes, a board does have to approve major corporate plans and actions.

MILLSTEIN: That's by law?

EISENBERG: No, by law it just has to approve dividends and so on.

MILLSTEIN: Virtually everything that's ever written tells boards what they ought to be doing, and it isn't dictated by legislation, and boards are doing it anyway. Now you don't need to go much beyond where we are now. They know what they're supposed to do.

EISENBERG: Here we are perhaps not in disagreement.

JEFF GORDON: There may be very big costs associated with requiring the auditing staff [Mel Eisenberg] proposed, both monetary and otherwise. In light of what Jill Fisch was saying about flexibility and costs and benefits and what Ira Millstein was saying about board responsibility, what are your views, Professor Eisenberg, on having such a staff to enable the board to do what you describe it should do?

EISENBERG: I am not talking about legal rules at the moment. I am not talking about statutes which say the board has to have responsibility for internal controls or how it's to be executed, because I agree with some of the things that have been said. For example, the publicity thing—I think the corporate culture aspect is really more important.

I think practice and theory were moving together in this reconceptualization of the board. And I think when you get a corporate culture which accepts certain norms, that's really probably more important than legal rules. So, number one, I'm just talking about, as I say, rules of corporate culture that I would like to see in place at the moment.

Having said that, I guess I would like to see a rule of corporate culture that, at least where you have an internal auditing staff, has them report to the board. I do not have data on the prevalence of internal audit staffs, and I may be incorrect in saying that most large publicly held corporations have them, although that's my impression from the empirical stuff I've seen.

## Current Commentary

"Most boards and executive teams welcome well-thought-through shareholder suggestions, and act in shareholders' best interest with deliberate speed. Everyone wins when boards and management work with sophisticated shareholders. In some regrettable cases, only the credible prospect of the 'flashlight'—typically a proxy contest—and the potential embarrassment from facts that light reveals, suffice to cause the incumbents to act. Shareholders should speak softly but carry a big flashlight!"

*–Paul Hilal*

MUNGER: If the Macey-Holdcroft proposal were adopted and the shareholders had an easy procedural way to force the sale of a corporation, you would find that at certain times practically every corporation in America was worth more to its shareholders sold out than continued. So, the proposals would just pass like crazy. It would be one of the most effective proposals ever adopted. So, when you examine the consequences of the proposal, you get a huge concentration.

Then if you carry it one step further—which any proper analysis would—you would examine the consequences of the consequences. And all the managers of American corporations—seeing the shareholders having this power to act in their own interest to force sell out after sell out—to prevent being displaced and so on, would go into great voluntary concentrations.

So, you're talking about a proposal with very profound macro consequences to the American economy and social system. Everybody would want to be so big that they'd have powerful interests in every congressional district and so forth, so the shareholders couldn't force a sell out merely because they were worth more sold out than continued as is. It would be a very shocking and powerful proposal, and I'm not sure if you really think through what would happen you would vote for it.

*Charlie Munger, Howard Buffett*

BUFFETT: As a stockholder, I'm really only interested in the board accomplishing two ends. One is to get a first class manager and the second is to intervene in some way when even that first class manager will have interests that are contrary to the interests of the owners.

I think there are great difficulties in achieving both of those ends. I've been a director of, counting them up, seventeen publicly owned companies, not counting ones which we control (which probably shows a very dominant, masochistic gene) (laughter). But over that time I've wrestled with just these couple of problems and there may be processes that would improve them.

The first one: getting the first class manager. I have never seen in those seventeen cases—and I'm not aware of it in other cases—where a question of mediocrity or worse and the evaluation of change has been made in the presence of a chief executive. It just doesn't happen. So, I think absolutely to have any chance of having that one solved, you have to have regular meetings of evaluation of chief executives, absent that chief executive.

If they are rump meetings or something of the sort—if they're not regularly scheduled—there is just too much tension created. Because a board may be a legal creation, but it's a social animal. It is very difficult for a group of people without a very strong leader to all of a sudden, spontaneously decide that they're going to hold some meetings elsewhere and discuss whether this person who may be a perfectly decent individual, really should be batting clean-up.

So, I think there should be a lot of emphasis on process in terms of evaluation of a CEO. I don't know how you create a greater willingness on the part of directors to really bounce somebody that they would bounce if they owned 100% of the company or if their family was dependent on the income from the business and so on. I just have not seen it in corporate America.

If you get that first class chief executive—which is a top priority—he doesn't have to be the best in the world, just a first class one. And I may agree with Jill to some extent—you may be able to turn a five into a five-and-a-half or something by having him consult with lots of other CEOs and get a lot of advice from the board. But my experience is that you don't turn a five into an eight. I think you're better off getting rid of the five and having him find something else to do in life and going out and acquiring an eight.

---

**Current Commentary**

"Buffett is famously savvy at finding first class chief executives for Berkshire's subsidiaries. In the two decades since the symposium, however, he has had to prove equally adept at replacing them when necessary, though usually without fanfare. While circumstances vary and little is said publicly, in that time CEO changes occurred at Benjamin Moore, Fechheimer Brothers, The Pampered Chef, Johns Manville, Larson Juhl, and NetJets. Notoriously, David Sokol, a Berkshire troubleshooter who ran its energy business and was widely seen as a potential successor to Buffett, resigned after buying stock in Lubrizol before pitching it as a Berkshire acquisition candidate."

*–Larry Cunningham*

The second problem is: even a first class chief executive has some interests that are in conflict with the shareholders. One is his or her own compensation. The second one gets into the acquisition category. There are psychic benefits to an executive of running a bigger show or just having more action or whatever that can be in conflict with the shareholders, even though that executive may be first class in other respects. The nature of acquisitions is that they get to the board at a point where if you turn them down you are rejecting the chief executive, you are embarrassing him in front of his troops, you're doing all kinds of things. So, it just doesn't happen.

I have seen board after board approve deals that afterwards the board members say, "you know, I really didn't think it was a very good idea but what could we do about it?" And there should be a better mechanism. But I'm not sure what it is. There should be a better mechanism, though, for a board to make those important decisions where a first class chief executive can have an absolutely different equation than the shareholders, weighing all of the personal economic and non-economic considerations.

There should be a mechanism that enables the board to bring independent judgment on those in a way that doesn't put the CEO in a position virtually where he or she has to resign or is embarrassed in front of the troops. And I would welcome any discussion on those matters.

The compensation question where the first class executive could be in conflict with the owners, I think it gets abused some but I don't think that it amounts to that much when compared with the other two questions—getting the right one and also the question of acquisitions. I think it costs shareholders some money that's unnecessary, and I think that a lot of the compensation schemes have been quite illogical, but I don't think that they are overwhelming in terms of evaluation.

KNOWLES: I just wanted to respond to two points Mr. Buffett made because they are useful. I think it's quite clear that the most important thing about process is to have it in place before problems emerge. Most lawyers know this and have to warn clients about it. Good corporate governance standards—like TIAA-CREF's and General Motors'—have that process in place.

On the second point, I think American corporate culture puts untoward faith in the law. We've done the exercise of comparing the various definitions of "independent director" and law students could write lots of papers on that. The New York Stock Exchange has one, TIAA-CREF has one, the American Law Institute has one—there are lots of definitions of "independent." But none of them get at the fact that humans are social animals and there's a whole set of values that the law cannot take into account.

Look at the range of definitions. Yet none of those definitions include being on charitable boards together, or with spouses on charitable boards together, or being scout leaders together, or the traditional example of playing golf together. And so unless the independence standards are taken with the limited value that I think they have—we all bow to them, we all insist on them—but we have to understand human nature and not put too much faith in the law to hedge around these dangers.

MILLSTEIN: As far as acquisitions and mergers are concerned, the general consensus seems to be that if the board learns its business—which is rare enough these days—but if the board really learns its business—and, by the way indoctrination and learning the business is something we at the National Association of Corporate Directors also recommend heavily—and then gets involved in the strategic plan and business plan in a much deeper way, emergency acquisitions and spur of the moment "good ideas" are much less likely to be brought to the board. Because if a board does contribute to an intelligent strategic plan and business plan, it's planning ahead on what it intends to do. And if it decides—it and management decide—to make an acquisition, it should be planned in advance, not something that walked in yesterday and is voted on today.

BUFFETT: I would say that more dumb acquisitions are made in the name of strategic plans than any other. I would be very wary if a board went through some elaborate process where a strategic plan was reviewed in great detail and then they endorse it and then the management went on to make acquisitions and then they came and said, "but we made it in accord with a strategic plan."

MILLSTEIN: Your basic argument that aggrandizement of the corporate size is not the game is something that I wish everybody would believe. But the world isn't there yet, so size is still important. It has to do with compensation, jets, planes—all the other nice things that go along with being a big company. When we convince everybody that that isn't the right way to go. I'll leave that to you. You're making a pretty good track record.

BUFFETT: On jet plane abuse (we're getting closer to the plane business so I have to be a little careful) (laughter) and on compensation, I can turn purple in meetings.[1] But in the end, the big, dumb acquisitions are going to cost shareholders far, far more money than all of the other stuff.

\* \* \* \* \*

*Deborah DeMott argued that for relational investing to meet its promise, large minority block holders must be obliged act as fiduciary agents for other shareholders, which is neither prevailing law nor feasible practically, noting in passing that people often cite Berkshire as an exemplar of the relational investor.*

BUFFETT: Can I make one comment? There is nothing Deborah said that I disagree with. Charlie and I, to my knowledge, have never used the word "relational" in describing our investment strategy, either in print or at shareholder meetings or anywhere else. Charlie can you think of any?

MUNGER: No.

BUFFETT: We don't think of ourselves that way. We say we are trying to buy into businesses with excellent economics, run by honest and able people at a decent price. We buy very few securities, so we look at it as "focused" investing. But the relationship aspect is not a key part of the investment strategy at all.

We will tend to have big blocks because we've got a lot of money. We buy very few stocks, so that would be an aspect of it, and we stick around a long time. So we do get to know the people in the business.

---

1. Editor's Note: Berkshire was acquiring FlightSafety International at the time.

But we've never used that term. I don't know where I first saw it, but it may well have been used in marketing certain funds that were set up and pretended to copy us when they weren't really copying what we did at all (laughter). I think that's where it comes from. We don't really associate ourselves with it.

What we are looking for are exactly what we've been seeking for decades. When we had way smaller funds, it was the same thing. When we bought stocks twenty years ago, we bought relatively few stocks. We didn't end up as a percentage of the company as we do now because we did not have the funds. We tended to have about the same relationships, or lack of them—in some cases we never met the managements and in other cases we have known them well.

But I think that the term has come to mean something a little different than what we do. I think that also people have a commercial interest in associating with us because they're trying to market something that perhaps had large management fees attached to it (laughter). But to the casual observer it might look like the same thing. But I don't disagree with anything you said. Charlie has something to say, though.

MUNGER: I don't think it's true that there is such a thing as true relationship investing. I'll bet there is practically none of it. There is very little of the type the du Ponts gave when they went into General Motors. Common sense says we're like that in part, and it's true, we are like that in part. They went in for a long time, and they planned to be constructive, and I don't think they made the investment so they could sell paint, although they did sell some. And I think that General Motors was better for having the du Ponts there—way better.

But there's tons of relational investing in the venture capital partnerships serving on the edge of technology in the Silicon Valley. There's tons of it. I think they hope to be constructive, but they will also take action if they don't like what's going on. They have more complicated legal problems than we do. They're more active in the management. They're more interested in selling small blocks or buying more. They have way more of the problems that you're talking about.

BUFFETT: They're more interested in an exit-strategy. And if you're more interested in an exit-strategy, you're going to have more legal problems. We're looking for a non-exit-strategy. We want to go into things where we'll never want to exit. I mean it's very simple. But if you are in a situation where you are both active and looking for an exit-strategy, you're going to have more problems. You're going to have more conflicts.

**Current Commentary**

"Stock selection and portfolio management are the keys to investment success. Warren popularized the concept of "focus investing," a portfolio management approach that concentrates one's bets on those stocks that have the highest probability of beating the market over the long term."

*—Robert Hagstrom*

ED KITCH: Deborah, you tried to apply or discussed applying a model of a control block as an agent for the other shareholders in the context of the Berkshire portfolio companies, and correctly observed that under present law the model was inapplicable. But it did strike me that there is one company in which the control block holder has assumed an agency obligation for the other shareholders and that's Berkshire Hathaway itself. Because the letters repeatedly say that "we are partners vis-a-vis the other shareholders." And with that, that's enough to create a partnership relationship. And would you then conclude that as to Berkshire Hathaway itself, the control block does have the very obligations you are speaking of?

BUFFETT: Could I sell my control block at a premium to somebody and leave the rest of the shareholders behind?

DEMOTT: I think that Ed's observations actually are susceptible to two different lines of response. There is a venerable line of partnership cases in which persons assert that a partnership relationship exists to induce other people to do things, typically to extend credit. And I'm not sure that that's the consequence in the Berkshire Hathaway statements—

KITCH: These are in writing. It induced people to buy and hold shares of Berkshire Hathaway.

DEMOTT: We also know that current law does not—absent some very unusual circumstances—require the person who sells the control block to share the premium with other shareholders.

KITCH: I know of no other company in which a control block has actually said to the other shareholders that we are in a partnership together.

BUFFETT: If you had some thought that you might behave in that way, then it would be crazy to say things like that. That's obvious. You're weakening whatever factual case you would have obviously later on. So, if you were to have any intent of, in any way taking advantage of the other shareholders, it doesn't pay to go around saying things like we're partners and this is a partnership and all that (laughter).

MUNGER: If you say the law is that the controlling shareholder doesn't have to share the premium, I think that's probably true if you look at cases. But I can remember a couple of just horrible cases where the controlling shareholder sold to a known crook or a known disreputable type and got a premium because the other guy (the buyer) was going to behave terribly. That's why he was going to pay the premium. I would, if I were still practicing law, be willing to take one of those cases on a contingent fee. I do not consider that safe behavior because I don't think the hornbook law can be that you can sell your company to any jerk you want to for a premium.

*Ira Millstein, Warren Buffett, Sandy Gottesman,
Dean David Rudenstine*

# FINANCE AND INVESTING

*Bill Klein, Lynn Stout, Larry Cunningham, Charlie Munger, Bob Hamilton, Bill Bratton*

\* \* \* \* \*

*Bill Bratton discussed dividends and reinvestment policy and reviewed strategies to ameliorate suboptimal dividend and reinvestment policy, including mandatory payout, enhanced shareholder monitoring and stepped-up disclosure.*

BUFFETT: About a dozen years ago, we at Berkshire had a ballot in connection with our annual meeting—not as part of the official proxy statement but sent along with it—where we asked our shareholders to vote on various alternative dividend policies. And we had a high response and we gave them maybe either three or four choices. Would you advocate that for public companies?

BRATTON: That's an interesting question. You're just suggesting a poll to inform managers. That is a very intriguing prospect. I see nothing wrong with the poll.

BUFFETT: The poll presumably would be a precatory operation and it might well be—and probably would be—accompanied by management's view as to the recommended course. We didn't do that, but we probably gave a few hints over the years (laughter). I'm just curious as to what you might think the general experience would be among the S&P 500 and whether you think that it would lead to changes in behavior or do you think it would be a good thing?

CUNNINGHAM: What were the results of that poll? I would expect the shareholders probably said the dividend policy that you have in place is terrific, that it's working well, and that it's part of the Berkshire menu.

BUFFETT: That's right. It's a self-selected group of shareholders, at least for those who read English (laughter). We asked the same thing about our charitable contributions program in the same poll. We were interested in how the shareholders felt about the old policies. We had told them the reason for our dividend policy, but to some extent it was for information about how well we thought we'd gotten across the point.

We gave them a no-dividend and low-pay dividend (around 20%) option. Charlie and my votes didn't count. By shares I think we found about 93-94% agreed; maybe by number of shareholders it was 90% agreed with the policy. But it's a self-selected group. There is no question about that.

But a more interesting question would be, what would happen if you did it at a company that's paying out a third or something of the sort, if you gave them a choice between two thirds and zero?

I would mention one point that, in terms of our investing companies, we have no impact and have tried to have no impact on dividend policy. We have not tried to, in fact—there was one exception maybe twenty years ago, twenty-five years ago.

BRAD REED: [*Directed to Munger, who was chairing this panel.*] Would you please describe Wesco's dividend policy, and second, would you discuss briefly your views of the relative efficacy of stock repurchases as opposed to dividends?

MUNGER: Wesco's dividend policy is that which the minority shareholders prefer, at least the ones we know who invited us in. So, we are just deferring to the wishes of the very much minority shareholders. Now you can say, "that's eccentric," and you're right.

Regarding common stock repurchases, if you're getting more intrinsic value than your cash is worth, why, of course that gets to be very attractive as a use of corporate funds. Alternatively, if you have a better use for the funds in terms of the value you get than repurchase, you should use the alternative purpose.

Everything should be done in terms of opportunity cost. Opportunity cost is so simple. If you're going to make a new investment, your opportunity cost of the new investment is whatever the next best choice you have available is. Now, you go through life like that instead of with this gibberish (laughter), all I can say is it works better.

BUFFETT: At Berkshire, incidentally, we have about three or four 80%-plus owned subsidiaries where the balance is owned by a few people, as opposed to Wesco where the minority interest is owned by a great many people. In each case, we tell the owners of the 20% or less interest that they set the dividend policy. It's up to them. We have no tax consequences to us in terms of dividend policy, they have tax consequences. They have a lot of other considerations within families and all of that, and they set the dividend policy.

In effect we say, "if you join us and you keep 20% or less of your company, the dividend policy is more important to you than it is to us." Because if we leave excess money in the company that can't effectively be used in the business and therefore is employed in investments, the resulting profits from those investments may be subject to higher state income tax rates and may have some other disadvantages to us. But we say that, net, we're willing to make that agreement with them, and we've followed it for 15 years in certain companies and will keep following it. But we do not sit down annually and figure out what is best for Berkshire Hathaway in terms of that.

MUNGER: You will not find that in your economic models (laughter).

---

**Current Commentary**

"It will be interesting to see if negative interest rates affect Berkshire's dividend policy."

*—Shane Parrish, Farnam Street*

---

BILL KLEIN: At the aggregate level it is opportunity cost and then that brings us back to the question of whose opportunity cost? Is it some sort of abstract corporate notion of opportunity cost which in turn would require the assumption or at least the presumption that Berkshire Hathaway would retain all its earnings and then choose among the various alternative investments available to it? But you could then ask, well, wait a second now, why are we thinking about Berkshire Hathaway's opportunity costs rather than about the opportunity costs of our shareholders?

MUNGER: Because we're running Berkshire Hathaway.

KLEIN: Yes, but you also have the power to decide to distribute that money to the shareholders and then let them make the decision.

MUNGER: We told you when we'll do that. That's in all the Buffett letters.

BUFFETT: If it translates into more than a dollar of market value then they have the option of taking the full dividend out and getting more than the dollar than they would have gotten if we sent it to them directly to use in whatever opportunity is available to them.

MUNGER: The break point that I couldn't get from my question, we've given in Berkshire's case. We say our break point is when we get so we can't deliver more than a dollar of market value per dollar retained, we will start distributing the money to the shareholders instead of retaining it. That's our break point.

BUFFETT: We might distribute more than 100% of the earnings.

MUNGER: You're damn right.

QUESTION: Berkshire's share price implies to me that the share price was substantially undervalued over time, and the company had a fairly low debt level. Why didn't Berkshire repurchase stock over the course of its history when that would have been an attractive alternative? Were the other opportunities that great?

MUNGER: If you look at the other opportunities, they've looked pretty good (laughter). If you take 1973-74, I would argue that what we were buying elsewhere was quite remarkable.

BUFFETT: We wish you could use a more recent example, Charlie (laughter).

MUNGER: What you get elsewhere is not so good anymore either.

---

**Current Commentary**

"Berkshire has been undervalued for most of the past 50 years, invariably below twice book value. Compare that to a bond with an equivalent rate of return—a 19% coupon—which invariably trade above twice par. Why not Berkshire? For one, few investors ever believed Berkshire could keep it going. Worse, few understand the power of "float" or deferred taxes, which makes book a low estimate of Berkshire's intrinsic value. While Berkshire's current vast scale makes a 19% coupon too high, in today's low-interest rate world, Berkshire's stock price is still low compared to value. Berkshire remains underappreciated."

—*Mark Hughes, Lafayette Investments*

---

### Current Commentary

"Berkshire has benefitted from the reported high rate of return as computed from the inception to the present. This is an attribute of high rates of return in the early years when a relatively small amount of money was involved. As Berkshire has grown, its returns have gotten closer and closer to the average. But the inception to present rate of return calculation benefits from the fact that it is an average of the annual returns, and is not weighted by the amount of assets under management. My own view is that simply managing this very large enterprise without large losses is a significant achievement, but it does not sound as impressive as beating the market averages consistently."

*−Ed Kitch*

* * * * *

*Larry Cunningham reviewed modern finance theory and contrasted it with Buffett's philosophy. Munger, chairing the panel, challenged the validity of teaching modern finance theory, suggesting it was both "trivial and twaddle."*

MUNGER: Suppose I am running a big pension fund that has net cash flows coming in every year. Very, very long-term obligations. And I decide that what I will do is program a bunch of computers to keep the fund continuously invested in very high beta stocks, very volatile stocks. And my computers do that and they do that year after year for twenty years. When it's all done, do I have a performance that is two, three, four, five percentage points above the average performance of the stock market. Yes or no (laughter)?

LOU SIMPSON: Charlie, I think you asked a very interesting question. I know what my answer would be, but I would be interested in what your answer would be to that question. You run a high-beta portfolio in a black box and you have used all of the academic measurements of volatility. At the end of twenty years when you total up the results, what do you think you end up with?

MUNGER: If you talk about Berkshire, I think the result would be far less than what we get using our methods. And I am deeply suspicious of the idea that a strategy so simple would work to produce a large advantage. I think if people believe there would be a huge advantage— two to three percentage points per annum over twenty or thirty years— they should believe in the tooth fairy.

QUESTION: [*Directed to Munger/continued.*] You've been talking about what should be taught—referring to some of what Professor Bratton discussed as gibberish and what Professor Cunningham discussed as twaddle—

MUNGER: By the way, I like both these guys (laughter).

QUESTION: [*continued*] You had a conventional law school education yourself and yet you came out and became a very successful lawyer and working with Mr. Buffett all these years.

MUNGER: It doesn't do a positive harm (laughter).

QUESTION: [*continued*] What would you suggest should be taught then? You said you do things different in Berkshire than all these theories that are trying to put in perspective some kind of teaching model. What should be taught?

MUNGER: You have 150 pages in front of you, and we've worked pretty hard at laying it out.[2]

ED KITCH: As a member of the teaching profession, I would like to say a kind word for the trivial. My experience in the classroom has been that students often report that some of the most important things they learn are what seems to me are trivial, but are quite news to them. I remember that when I learned in class that a stock split was not really an important or beneficial event for shareholders, it was quite a revelation

---

2. Editor's Note: Symposium participants received a 150-page collection of Buffett's letters to Berkshire shareholders, subsequently revised and published as *The Essays of Warren Buffett: Lessons for Corporate America*.

to me. I think it's an utterly trivial proposition. But if you haven't heard of it, it's actually very useful to have someone tell you.

MUNGER: I would accept that and I would argue that what Berkshire has done has mostly been using trivial knowledge. And it's the fact that we concentrate so much on trivial knowledge that enables us to—

KITCH: Then would you advise our students that if they focus on the trivial points we're making, that in the end they may end up with several million dollars (laughter)?

MUNGER: Yes (laughter). I think the answer is that if you absorb the important basic knowledge—which at least for the best students is very easy to assimilate—and you absorb all the big basic points across a broad range of disciplines, one day you'll walk down the street and you'll find that you're one of the very most competent members of your generation, and that many people who were quicker mentally and worked harder are in your dust. So, yes, by all means teach the big important points. And the fact that they're nearly obvious, if they're important enough, you probably should even repeat them.

*Bill Ackman*

BILL ACKMAN: Volatility is a good measure of risk if you don't look at security price volatility, but at business volatility. For example, if you look at the businesses that Berkshire has invested in—like Gillette or Coke, businesses with a franchise that's impenetrable. These are businesses with underlying economics have very low volatility. And if you look at the consistent earnings I think that volatility is a good measure of risk. The problem is, looking at security price volatility is not a good measure of risk. And I think that the model should be adjusted to look at the underlying economics of the business as opposed to where pieces of paper trade and exchange on a daily basis.

CUNNINGHAM: Right, and that implicates the efficiency assumption. There would be a direct link between underlying business volatility and stock price volatility if the efficiency hypothesis were true.

MUNGER: Isn't it true that a lot of the confusion comes from people saying risk, which had an ordinary conventional meaning before these financial types grabbed the word, and they don't really mean risk in a conventional sense, they mean volatility.

---

**Current Commentary**

"One of the top ten lessons from Warren and Charlie is understanding the difference between business volatility and stock price volatility. Along the way, academics kidnapped these two terms in the name of efficient market hypothesis. Being businessmen, Warren and Charlie never bowed to the Ivory Tower theorists and that has made all the difference."

*–Robert Hagstrom*

---

CUNNINGHAM: Yes, they mean stock price volatility, not business volatility either.

BUFFETT: When beta measures volatility—or relative volatility I should say—to then make a jump and call it risk—they ought to, throughout the entire literature when beta is talked about, just say "relative volatility." I think it would bring a whole different complexion to the argument.

CUNNINGHAM: I think that's right and I think it comes back—all this ultimately comes back—to the efficiency story: that stock prices fully and accurately reflect all relevant information about the security.

MUNGER: How could anybody really believe that? You could believe that it's roughly so with the important variations, but how could anybody believe that it was strictly so?

CUNNINGHAM: That's why proponents respond with breaking the efficiency story into three versions: the strong form, semi-strong form and the weak form. And there are a lot of people who believe in the semi-strong form.

MUNGER: We believe in the weak form.

---

**Current Commentary**

"Berkshire's investment behavior repeatedly demonstrates the value of knowing the difference between business volatility and stock market volaitity. Amid the financial crisis that began in 2008, for example, while many were paralyzed, Berkshire made numerous lucrative investments, including in Bank of America, General Electric, and Goldman Sachs."

*—Larry Cunningham*

---

*Larry Cunningham, Charlie Munger*

\* \* \* \* \*

*Bob Hamilton explored Berkshire's 1996 recapitalization, designed to thwart efforts to market Berkshire shares, then priced in excess of $30,000, at a low price that would increase trading, by offering a new class B with fractional voting and economic rights that would trade at a lower price. Hamilton read Berkshire's prospectus disclosure, including cautionary statements from Buffett and Munger that Berkshire stock was not undervalued and they would not buy Berkshire stock at current prices.*

MUNGER: It is an interesting story. You can argue that it demonstrates an important principle of law: you don't want the judges running the prisons or the detailed operations of the corporations of America or whatnot, and yet you want certain standards of behavior that are so awful that you want judges or legislatures to intervene.

Between that intervention point and the best possible behavior should be a big area, and you want a big area where it isn't illegal in the sense that courts will intervene, but where you allow room for a lot of behavior that's a lot better than the minimum standards. And I would argue that this prospectus was just an example of behavior that was better than the minimum standards of the civilization, and to the extent that anybody wants to make it an example for law students or anybody else, I encourage it.

QUESTION: With respect to pricing of stock, what would be the effect if Mr. Buffett died? How would you expect Berkshire's stock price to react?

HAMILTON: It will have an effect, that's for sure. And it would probably be, at least temporarily, very negative.

MUNGER: This is not a subject that one of our members likes exploring (laughter).

BUFFETT: It won't be as negative for the holders as it will be for me (laughter).

\* \* \* \* \*

*Lynn Stout explained a model of stock market behavior, which instead of assuming purely rational actors, embraces the possibility of varied participants with different assessments and beliefs.*

MUNGER: Lynn, what is your personal opinion of those people who would expect inefficiencies (mispricing) to occur because of certain standard cognitive defects of humankind?

STOUT: They're right.

MUNGER: I certainly agree with that and that means you have to listen to psychologists if you want to predict standard patterns of irrationality, doesn't it?

STOUT: This is the problem of the mathematician-economist versus the natural science-economist. One of the reasons that efficient market theory in its conventional sense rose to the pinnacle that it did, was there was a group of economists who really wanted to be mathematicians and it gave them a chance to play with Greek letters and show what good mathematicians they were.

In the process they forgot the natural scientist's [mission] which is that you ought to try to come up with models that actually predict what happens in the world. And if in fact you want to come up with models that predict what happens in the world then, yes, indeed we should be listening to the psychologists.

MUNGER: So we really have an extreme example here of a lot of nonsense which is created by the psychological phenomenon in the proverb: "To the man with a hammer every problem tends to look like a nail."

BILL ACKMAN: We've heard a lot of discussion about how institutions and individuals use index funds. But to the extent that more and more capital becomes indexed—and if you think about index fund managers as really being a computer, then in terms of the voting of shares for instance—the more stock that is held by people who don't care about individual corporations, the more there is a significant societal detriment to have capital in the hands of people who are just seeking average performance. The result is that the more capital that is indexed, the more it inflates the prices of companies in the S&P 500 and leads to poor capital allocation and maybe detrimental owner performance over time because some companies get more capital than they deserve.

MUNGER: You are plainly right. If you pushed indexation to the very logical extreme you would get preposterous results.

STOUT: But, empirically, the portion of equity capital assets that are indexed is less than thirty percent of the total.

ACKMAN: That's what is officially indexed. There is an enormous amount of capital that is unofficially indexed.

MUNGER: It's called closet indexation: you keep the fee but you deliver the index.

GORDON: But there is no necessary connection between indexing and bad corporate governance. CalPERS [California Public Employees' Retirement System] has a huge index fund but it is very vigorous about corporate governance precisely because it says, "we aren't going to sell—we are in there for the long term." They are a bit like Charlie and Warren in that respect. They say, "we are in it for the long term and therefore we have to look at the companies that are underperforming and see what we can do to fix them in their index fund."

So, in fact, there is an argument that having ownership through financial intermediaries that are indexed is a far more effective means of corporate governance than having shares owned by individual shareholders for whom collective action problems of corporate governance intervention are overwhelming.

MUNGER: Well, ladies and gentleman you have just heard a very subtle and profoundly correct point.

OESTERLE: A quick response to Lynn Stout on takeover premiums. Assuming that you are correct that the inframarginal shareholder determines the ultimate takeover premium, that still leaves you with one takeover price—the one takeover price of the inframarginal shareholder—that gives a lot of windfall gains to everyone else so you still have a net social gain even under your theory.

Point two: the inframarginal shareholder's position on why they are optimistic—your argument is circular. Why they are optimistic might be related to the power of the bargaining process that they have vis-à-vis bidders. So, I could be that inframarginal shareholder and believe that we can extract the last dollar from this bidder and that's the reason I'm so optimistic and demand the premium. So, your argument doesn't explain much to me, and I think it's circular.

## Current Commentary

"It was Charlie who educated the Berkshire faithful on the dangers of cognitive defects in decision making, now popularly referred to as behavioral finance. If you want to best understand the source of mispricing, study and listen to the psychologists."

—*Robert Hagstrom*

STOUT: There is a rational expectations aspect to the tussle between the bidder and the target and I think you're right that part of that is going to potentially cause some inflation in the value that is attached by the target once they know the bidder is interested. But since bidders do have other options and since they won't pay infinite prices and target shareholders know that, even though that is a feedback mechanism, the argument is not circular. That is one more factor, but it does not destroy the basic point.

I agree completely with your first observation which is that, if in fact the takeover bidder paid the premium price of the most optimistic shareholder in the firm to every shareholder in the firm that would clearly be a source of large social gain, at least measured ex ante.

Where the puzzle comes up for me is the interesting case—which is not unusual—where the firm does not pay the reservation price of the most optimistic investor but pays the reservation price of the investor who owns the fifty-first percentile—they go up the curve enough to buy the first half. So, the people in the first half of the curve, many of them get a benefit. Unfortunately, the people on the last part of the curve will, under conventional state merger rules, often be forced out at a price they deem is too low. So, actually measuring the gain when you are setting the price by the fifty-first percentile becomes much messier and I am very agnostic in those situations.

MUNGER: If you have a corporation 100% owned by one owner and he holds an auction, don't you often get a very irrationally high price?

STOUT: Winner's curse?

MUNGER: Yes.

STOUT: Yes.

MUNGER: And that doesn't have anything to do with your explanation.

STOUT: It is related. You can't have a winner's curse unless you presume that people disagree. I flog the heterogeneous expectations theory because in part it is a useful way to get people started down the road of looking at phenomena like the winner's curse.

MUNGER: Can't you get a winner's curse when you've got a whole lot of bidders competing? One says: After all, it's worth 100 to the other guy, and I've already decided to do it, so why not bid 101? And the other guy thinks, well, it's worth 101 to him. Don't you get a psychological process that creates a lot of social proof and a lot of idiocy that really isn't related to normal supply and demand curves?

STOUT: Personally I stay away from Sotheby's.

MUNGER: It's psychological idiocy you are fearing.

STOUT: Yes.

MUNGER: We don't go to auctions either.

MUNGER: Lynn, if you were playing bridge and you announced that your strategy was going to be to count the diamonds and hearts but not the spades and clubs, would you consider that a rational way to play bridge?

STOUT: Well I'm at a tremendous disadvantage here because I've been too busy figuring out Greek letters to learn bridge. But assuming it's like other card games, if I were to do that I think that wouldn't be too sensible.

MUNGER: If the world is multidisciplinary, does it make sense to explain these occurrences solely in terms of economics without any psychology?

STOUT: Use the right tool for the job.

MUNGER: But isn't reality multidisciplinary, so that you have to use the tools of all the disciplines to solve the complex problems?

STOUT: Yes, and be willing to pick and choose depending on which seem to work best.

MUNGER: But you can't have a whole area where you say, "I don't carry that tool kit and just do the best with what I've got." That isn't too rational a way to handle it is it?

STOUT: I'm guilty.

MUNGER: We all are.

GORDON: But Charlie, at the end of the day, you don't expect your shareholders to ask whether they are happy. You ask them to look at the bottom line. *The Buffett Essays* are all about essentially focusing on ways to bring economic reality to bear on the running of a business. Insofar as psychology enters the picture it is something to be avoided, driven out and hopefully patiently waded through.

MUNGER: Driven out of supervising a bunch of subordinate managers? Psychology driven out? How?

GORDON: You're dealing with people to be sure, but in making investments don't you try to weight out the psychology before you buy?

MUNGER: Yes, we don't go to auctions. I'm like Lynn, I'm afraid of my own idiocy.

**Current Commentary**

"To solve complex problems, Charlie tells us to be multidisciplinary in our thinking. The introduction of the major mental models into the world of investing may be Charlie's single greatest contribution for helping individuals become better investors."

*–Robert Hagstrom*

# MERGERS AND
# ACQUISITIONS

*Dale Oesterle, Jim Cox, Larry Cunningham,*
*Jeff Gordon, Charles Yablon*

\* \* \* \* \*

*Jeff Gordon examined comments Buffett made in 1985 about giving shareholders the ultimate decision whether to sell compared to recent cases where courts deferred to director decisions to sell even when director independence was doubtful. To begin the colloquy, Professor Gordon asked if that made sense to Buffett, as well as the following questions.*

GORDON: I have two [other] questions for Warren Buffett. First, do you still retain your skepticism about the independence of directors in the context of a corporation faced with a hostile bid, and if so, what do you think about the Delaware jurisprudence and the current corporate law reforms that rely on them? Second: with merger and acquisition activity now at a record high—mostly through stock-for-stock exchanges—how do you feel about this in light of your concern about the casino society and the potentially debased consideration that stock might well become?

BUFFETT: I would say my views on the ones you quoted from 1985 are still very close to where I am. I mean my heart still does belong to the shareholder. I see problems with negotiated value where you get a situation like 1974 where there wasn't a company I know of that wasn't selling at half of its negotiated value or less and there would have been a turnover at the very best companies en masse and every shareholder behaving in their rational interest. That bothers me but I don't have any great answer for it, and in the end, I come back to the shareholder.

I think the directors are far from independent judges of the merits of an unsolicited tender offer. So they are far from the best solution. But Charlie is probably more familiar with the cases than I am.

MUNGER: This is one of the rare occasions where Warren and I have a very slight difference of opinion. I am less troubled by not allowing just a cascade of acquisitions in America. I totally agree that for the ordinary little family that owns a theater, that the shareholders ought to decide whether the theater is sold. But once you get into great big social institutions that, given certain laws, will cascade in waves of acquisitions and huge agglomerations, that bothers me enough. So, I think that it's appropriate to have laws in the civilization that prevent it.

**Current Commentary**

"It is remarkable how rarely Warren and Charlie have expressed differences of opinion on business policy, particularly given their political differences, with Warren slightly left of center and Charlie slightly right. But Warren hints often about the great value of their more frequent differences of opinion over Berkshire acquisition decisions, as Charlie vetoed so many ideas Warren believed in that Warren dubbed him the 'abominable no man.' "

*–Larry Cunningham*

QUESTION: Do you think most stockholders have the ability to make an assessment about a sale? For example, if you look at the balance sheet of a corporation and you see large amounts of fixed assets that are carried at cost less accumulated depreciation that might differ significantly from current market value, or you look at the income statement and there are other factors where there could be some difficulty on the part of most people in trying to make an assessment. And it would appear to me that of the millions of shareholders who are just buying hoping that the stock will go up, that most of them lack the ability to make an adequate determination.

GORDON: For myself—and I think I find support in this in some of *The Buffett Essays*—a legal rule that relies on the incompetence or gullibility of shareholders seems to me improbable. We let people buy stock without a license and in the ordinary course they can sell it too. So the starting point that shareholders are unable to assess a bid coming over the transom against their hopes and expectations for the company in which they buy stock and the stock price, it just seems to me a slightly strange view given that we let shareholders buy stock and sell it in the ordinary course.

BUFFETT: Let me postulate this. Company A, a very large company, is selling at $100 a share. Company B is some rather smaller company selling at $80 a share. Company A decides that there are benefits of joining up with Company B so they offer a share-for-share exchange.

Company B shareholders are happy they're going to get $100 a share for this deal and they vote it and the investment bankers bless it, et cetera.

And say that extra value presumably comes from the synergy that would be achieved from putting these two entities together. The market is efficient, we'll say, about evaluating each one on their own, but putting them together creates enough synergy so that an efficient market also will say that the resulting company is worth $102, just to pick a figure.

Now let's turn it inside out and assume that Company A's directors are sitting in a director's meeting one day and in come Company B's investment bankers and they say, we'll offer one share of Company B (the $80 stock) for every share of Company A (the $100 stock). If that transaction went through it would have exactly the same number of shares outstanding, the same business economies of the two and everything else.

But I think you will find no one who would say that Company A's shareholders with stock at $100 a share should accept this $80 a share, although presumably it would be worth $102 just the same way, because the same number of shares would be outstanding, the same economies would be realized, and so on. What should the director's behavior be in both of those illustrations?

GORDON: In the first case, if I'm following this correctly, the acquirer is in effect paying the shareholders of the target a premium in the value of the stock.

BUFFETT: Taking one share of this new Company AB, which presumably will sell at least at the price of Company A stock which was $100. How should Company A's directors feel about making that offer assuming that the synergies are real and everything else? Do you have any problem with that?

GORDON: At the end of the day the shareholders of the target company are going to end up with stock that it is reasonable to believe will be greater in value than the stock that they are now holding. That would seem to be a move that the directors could reasonably approve of.

BUFFETT: I'm focusing though primarily here on Company A's directors in approving this offer.

GORDON: You mean Company A's directors having $100 a share stock offering it in a stock-for-stock exchange for $80?

BUFFETT: Right.

GORDON: It could be that they have a view that Company B's stock is in fact undervalued in the use for which Company A might put it. And so, therefore, assuming that there are going to be synergy gains associated, it's not unreasonable to give to the shareholders of B a disproportionate share of those synergy gains in order to get the B company board to agree to go along with the acquisition.

BUFFETT: Let's say B walks in and offers the same share of this combined AB, but B just happens to be the acquirer now and A is the target company. How do you think the A directors should respond? Same exact facts of operations.

GORDON: Except in that case the A shareholders have a $100 per share stock and they're being offered stock that's $80 a share with the speculation that the stock they'll end up with is $102 a share. I would be a little bit nervous in exchanging something that I know is $100 a share for something that might be worth $102 a share, but knowing that, essentially, I'm for sure getting something that the market has valued at only $80 a share.

*Jeff Gordon*

BUFFETT: You know the deal isn't going to go through for a month or two months or something of the sort, by the time it gets all through winding its way through the shareholder votes and Hart-Scott-Rodino. What I am just trying to determine is whether the identical transaction should get a different response from the A Company board.

GORDON: If A is moving forward, then presumably I guess what you're saying is that, if A then satisfies itself, the A board has the same certainty in both cases that there will be the realized synergy gains. It's a very interesting case (laughter). The problem is that it might be hard to persuade the shareholders that, in fact, the two cases are the same case.

BUFFETT: The second case would change B's name to A after the merger (laughter).

MUNGER: Warren's second class of cases is a very interesting case. It's what I call a null class—it has no members (laughter).

BUFFETT: But it illustrates either that the market is not efficient or directors will behave differently based on whether they are the acquiring company or the target company.

FISCH: Just in case you think that Mr. Buffett's second hypothetical is farfetched, there really is a class. The recent Chase-Chemical merger bears a striking resemblance to that second scenario in which the $80 stock is being given to the stockholders that had $100 stock. Clearly you have a synergy there, but distribution of gains and whether the directors should have gone forward with that raises precisely this issue.

GORDON: Let me ask one of Mr. Buffett (laughter). What about what I see as a wedge between intrinsic value—which we understand what you mean by that—and negotiated value—which I'm not sure what you mean by that or what the connection is with intrinsic value or whether it troubles you that negotiated value might be higher than intrinsic value.

BUFFETT: Negotiated value is where a transaction will take place today under all the normal economic assumptions and circumstances—a willing buyer and a willing seller, et cetera. Intrinsic value can differ materially from negotiated value. Negotiated value represents hopes and fears and intrinsic value—admittedly, no one is going to know it precisely.

But the intrinsic value is if the company itself were a bond and you could see all the coupons printed out between now and judgment day, if you discounted those back at government bond rates since you would know the certainty, the same certainty that you would have on a government bond what that number would be. Those numbers differ. I would say that now negotiated values on balance relative to intrinsic values are probably higher than they were ten or fifteen years ago, but that's just a function of the different kind of environment we're in. They move around a lot over time.

GORDON: But does it trouble you? In your 1985 remarks you seemed to be thinking that it was a problem that tender offers were—

BUFFETT: In 1974, for example, I would have said it was a problem that negotiated values would have been below intrinsic values. It's a problem for us in buying businesses now when negotiated values may be above intrinsic values. But in terms of the societal problem, the fact that every management—no matter what kind of a job it has done—gets turned out, they're going to get turned out in a time when negotiated values are well below intrinsic values. It just means that an auction market is underpricing assets—good, bad or indifferent—and I don't like the consequences of that in terms of what it means for what I would call an orderly, well-developed management of businesses over time.

## Current Commentary

"Berkshire's acquisition strategy is distinct: never hostile, usually all cash, and often below intrinsic value as sellers accept less economic consideration because they attribute value to the intangibles of Berkshire culture, including managerial autonomy and a commitment to permanent ownership."

*—Larry Cunningham*

* * * * *

*Dale Oesterle defended as neglected national assets the raiders in leveraged cash acquisitions of the 1980s by showing that they produced substantial net social gains but were allocated less than their share of those gains due to various federal and state laws.*

GORDON: Dale, a couple of questions. First, given that M&A activity is in fact at a historical high right now, what does that say to the essentially empirical claim you're making that the set of constraints has inhibited bidder activity below some optimal level?

OESTERLE: The kind of bidders that I'm looking at are cash bidders in leveraged acquisitions. They are not in this new wave. You don't have a lot of cash bidders and you don't have high leverage in a lot of these new acquisitions. What we have is stock swaps, and the reason we have a lot of stock swaps is because the stock market is at an all-time high. And my explanation of that is, when you're dealing with stock swaps you don't disadvantage bidders to the extent that you do in cash offers.

So, to the extent that high stock prices go away and we don't have the advantage of using stock in acquisitions, whether or not you'll see a resuscitation of the cash market in leveraged acquisitions is really up for grabs. I think you've disadvantaged bidders in the stock swaps too, but the degree of the disadvantage is not nearly as substantial as it is in the cash offers, particularly because the Williams Act doesn't have the impact that it has in these stock swaps.

*Dale Oesterle*

GORDON: Let's distinguish between hostile bidders and other bidders because it seems that in the context of the stock swap where you're resulting in a merger of equals, in fact, the parties together can create barriers to the incursion by a third party that preserves more of the gains for the first bidder than under the open market auction regime. So, why not say that things are going just fine, even with respect to the appropriate incentive for bidders?

OESTERLE: This is where you and I disagree. In the *Time-Warner* line of cases, you're worrying about Time [whereas] I worry about Warner. And if you take it from the perspective of Warner, you have a different take. Again, the stock swap cases represent a different case. I think bidders are simply less disadvantaged in stock swap cases which are usually statutory mergers that have full shareholder votes. You don't get too many stock tender offers in these acquisitions. You're talking about the difference between a statutory merger and a cash tender offer, and that's where the impact is.

GORDON: Dale, let me ask you to address Charlie Munger's comment earlier which is his concern about the cascade effect associated with an unregulated market in corporate control. Notwithstanding the level of regulation that obtained throughout most of the '80s, there was a high degree of activity. What shut it down was probably the collapse of the junk bond market which wasn't necessarily for regulatory reasons. Are you at all concerned that moving in the direction that you want would lead to the cascade that Charlie sees as socially concerning?

OESTERLE: Charlie, I don't know how to handle a question like that because it seems to me, cascades are always bad, I guess, unless you're talking about rivers and waterfalls. It seems to me that acquisitions are good if you create value for people who are participants in them and they're not so good if you don't. And the number in any given period is almost irrelevant.

In periods where you have tremendous technological change—which is I think a description of the '80s, as a lot of industries were moving very fast in the '80s and incumbent managers were simply not keeping up— that you would expect to see a lot of acquisitions. And in a period where you didn't have a lot of industry change, you wouldn't expect to see a lot of acquisitions. But it seems to me that the quality of the acquisitions are what you're looking at and not the number in any period of time. Am I being unfair to your point there?

MUNGER: Take the simple case of the current era. Does society have any interest in how much horizontal combination there is? Assume stocks go up another 50% and the Justice Department standards are relaxed, which is what they are now. They allow huge amounts of horizontal activity. If you say, I just look at the stock market and I see shareholders getting quotational changes after each transaction, therefore there's a lot of social good, I don't follow you.

I say, the social good takes a much wider calculus. And there are very interesting questions about how much horizontal combination the world wants. And I don't come to a perfect conclusion on this, but there are dangers that I see going on in my head.

On the other side though, I see a whole lot of financial promoters getting very rich with soft, white hands, and their major contribution is to sell one division to a competitor and squeeze a little blood out of another. And that may be socially desirable and it may not.

BUFFETT: Which side do you come down on (laughter)?

MUNGER: Generally, I'm not in favor of a social system which throws just huge rewards to people who invent nothing, don't improve the factories or don't invent better systems and so forth. Of course, you can argue that I'm condemning myself (laughter). All I can say is it's almost intentional.

---

**Current Commentary**

"This discussion addressed "promoters," not financial intermediaries, which may be more prominent now in 2016."

—*Deborah DeMott*

---

OESTERLE: The antitrust concerns are real, but it's a separate issue. Whether or not you should allow mergers within the same industry, we have an antitrust law, how it's interpreted is sort of what our elected officials are supposed to do for us. They can get it right or wrong. But it seems to me regulating the division of gains between bidders and targets ought to be neutral of your antitrust policy unless your antitrust policy is so infirm that this is sort of a second best solution to a decent antitrust policy.

MUNGER: That would be a pretty good idea.

OESTERLE: I hope that's not true. I haven't given up on antitrust.

MUNGER: Then you don't have a sufficiently cynical view of human nature (laughter).

## Current Commentary

"The point I made in my discussions with Mr. Munger still stands. We have too many laws that interfere with leveraged acquisitions. They do not stop them, but they affect how parties split the gains. Target firm shareholders still take the lion's share of the acquisitions profits. This has many effects. The laws discourage bidders, encourage target boards to spend substantial resources discouraging acquisition offers and/or shareholder requests, and stimulate a hedge fund industry to spend funds to overcome the stubborn resistance of reluctant boards. Even brokered government bailouts are made more likely. These are all social losses."

*—Dale Oesterle*

\* \* \* \* \*

*Chuck Yablon explored the role of corporate culture in mergers, speculating that Buffett regards personal character as a significant factor in culture and referencing contemporary takeover cases, including Time-Warner. Yablon then supposed that Buffett's approach to takeovers is similar to that of Delaware law, including board responses akin to that in Time-Warner, such as rejecting a much higher all cash bid in favor of a stock-for-stock merger or in favor of a bid of half cash and half stock. He imagined Buffett as a Justice on the Delaware Supreme Court and posed three questions about a hypothetical hostile takeover scenario.*

YABLON: Three basic questions: Did the target management engage in a reasonable deliberative process? Does their conclusion that white knight's deal offers more long-term value for shareholders make economic sense in light of known and reasonably anticipated business positions? And, three, have the people on the target's board shown themselves to be trustworthy in the way they have comported themselves in this and prior business situations?

It is only if all three of these criteria can be shown to be satisfied by a preponderance of the evidence I submit, that Justice Buffett will be likely to uphold management's decision to resist the higher cash offer. I also submit they are not a bad set of criteria to apply in such situations, and who knows, they could even be Delaware law (laughter).

BUFFETT: The equity component makes it very tough, particularly if you have taxpaying shareholders who might be able to get a tax-free exchange on the second half. So, the cash offer I think is fairly easy to decide. I think you really do get into judgment in the case you postulated with equity. I could see myself as a shareholder of the target preferring either case depending on the specific prospects of the acquiring company's stock and depending on the tax basis of a great many of the shareholders. So, I think I could go either way in the case involving equity securities.

MUNGER: But do you want the Delaware Supreme Court to use its brilliant judgment about investment performance and make that decision, or do you want to say, this is within the business judgment rule?

YABLON: Or do you create some kind of enhanced business judgment where the Delaware Court asks fairly searching questions about how management conducted their investigation to reach the conclusion?

BUFFETT: Having seen the process, I worry about relying on it (laughter).

MUNGER: The process of hiring experts who follow the rule of "Whose bread I eat, his song I sing," and then relying on that—if the Delaware Supreme Court thinks that's the right way to rule, well, they're wrong.

BUFFETT: If I'm going to pay $5 million to somebody if they give me the advice and the deal goes through, then I think I probably ought to pay $5 million to somebody else whose advice I listen to who gets paid the $5 million only if the deal doesn't go through (laughter).

GORDON: Except, actually, I thought what Justice Buffett said was actually at variance with the rule you propose because what I heard [him] say is that, it ought to be a matter of shareholder choice. And the problem that we see with target defensive tactics is that it is precisely in respect to the board's decision to take the matter away from shareholder choice that the legal issue gets joined.

YABLON: Although what Justice Buffett just said was, sometimes shareholder choice doesn't work precisely because different shareholders may have different preferences with respect to the same offer. If the offers are close enough, then the question is do you defer to a management decision?

*Charles Yablon*

BUFFETT: Assume there were a takeover offer for Berkshire. Close to 90% of our shares are held by people with a tax basis of under $100 a share (laughter). They might have different feelings about weighing two different offers, one of which constituted a security they were perfectly happy to continue owning and which was tax-free, versus one which was 5% higher for cash.

GORDON: That's true assuming that there were a shareholder choice in the matter. Why not assume that shareholders would make the rational choice as opposed to, and this is the rub, leaving it to Berkshire's board to essentially fend off the choice that, on your hypothesis the shareholders would dis-prefer anyway?

BUFFETT: I would not like it if the directors made a decision that 90% of the shareholders were unhappy with. They presumably might get to act on that too.

GORDON: Okay, so it sounds to me like if I'm maybe putting words in your mouth, that Justice Buffett rejects the proposed standard, because again it substitutes some set of procedures, tests, judgments made by the target directors over the same weighing and balancing made by the target shareholders.

MUNGER: I'm not sure if that's totally right (laughter). Think that through from the viewpoint of the corporation that is making the merger offer, half cash, half stock. Now if that automatically triggers an auction where the company is simply knocked down to the highest bidder, who in the hell wants to be in those transactions? So, again, if you think through the consequences of a rule of law carefully enough, you're likely to come to some conclusions about what the appropriate rule is. I regard those consequences as quite pernicious.

A rule of law that says, I can't go out and say half cash and half stock without triggering an auction—I would regard that as a very silly rule of law and I'm not at all sure that it's the law of Delaware. I think maybe the corporation can make that kind of merger and put the thing to vote and carry it all the way through whether it's voted down or not, and I think he could bind himself not to listen to anybody else until the whole voting process was over. The other person can say we're going to make a cash offer if you turn us down.

YABLON: They'd probably have to do some listening.

MUNGER: What?

YABLON: I think they'd probably have to do some listening to alternative offers.

MUNGER: Do some what?

YABLON: I don't think they could bind themselves not to listen to alternative offers.

MUNGER: I think they could bind themselves to let the shareholders decide and not to listen to anything else until the vote is over. At least I've written a contract that said that (laughter).

# ACCOUNTING AND TAXATION

*Cal Johnson, Ed Kitch, Lou Lowenstein, Elliott Weiss, Jim Repetti*

\* \* \* \* \*

*Elliott Weiss discussed the accessibility of The Buffett Essays, especially for students learning accounting and valuation, including to develop an understanding of the limits and malleability of these tools.*

BUFFETT: What bothers me, in addition to everything that has just been enumerated, is that I see the auditors encouraging it. And I say to myself: There are only six of you who have to get together and agree we're not going to play around this way and there will be a stigma attached to anyone that has a certificate from anyone but those six.[3] So it doesn't require some huge brave act of the auditing profession to get better financial reporting. But it doesn't happen and in effect they become conspirators.

There is no question the leeway I have to report earnings as CEO of Berkshire is enormous. I don't know how to quantify it precisely, and some of it would catch up with you later on, in terms of insurance reserves, for example. In an insurance company, the long-tail business in particular, you can paint any picture you want, for a period that probably encompasses enough time to either buy out the public or to effect a major public offering.

SIMPSON: On the question of pooling and protecting pooling by satisfying the technical requirements—the implication to me is that companies think the market is stupid and they really don't look at real economics, but only the purely cosmetic accounting of it. Maybe this is naive, but I think the market does, over some period of time, look at real economic earnings and that companies are fooling themselves if they think that they can do all these cosmetic accounting things and have the market believe it. Am I naive?

MUNGER: I can answer that in part, sharing my love of biology and psychology. They've done very interesting experiments with monkeys in zoos. They create a system where the monkey can do things to get a token and the token can immediately be exchanged for a banana. The monkey soon learns to work just as hard for a token as he formerly did for a banana. You can hardly think that corporate managements are going to be much better (laughter).

BUFFETT: In certain kinds of markets—including in the late 1960s for sure and maybe some more recently—there is a feeling among people who are either very smart or cynical that they would rather buy into manipulated earnings than real earnings because there is more certainty of manipulated earnings coming through on target for some time and they will get out before it all collapses. I saw that first hand in the sixties.

---

3. Editor's Note: In 1996, the auditing profession was dominated by six major firms and soon shrank to four, thanks to the 1998 merger of Price Waterhouse and Coopers & Lybrand and the 2002 dissolution of Arthur Andersen.

There are people who think it is rational to play along with a game that isn't going to be discovered until they are out of it. I would say that I agree with Lou [Simpson] practically all the time, but a lot of money can change hands during the period of manipulation before it eventually tarnishes the reputation of the National Student Marketings of the world.

LOU LOWENSTEIN: Arthur Wyatt, a very distinguished accountant at Arthur Andersen, reported some years ago on off-balance sheet financing. At Supermarkets General, we paid hard cash to push financing off the balance sheet—before I became President. It's endemic. The debt is there but we don't want it on the balance sheet. There was a study that he reported on: 40% of the securities analysts—and maybe more importantly of loan officers—missed the off-balance sheet financing. If you can fool 40% of the people all the time, that's not bad.

At GE, Jack Welch is ever devoted to increasing earnings-per-share. One year, earnings were really down except for an adjustment to the assumptions under the pension plan and the liquidation of a LIFO reserve which very conveniently produced up earnings instead of down earnings. Of nine securities analyst reports, only one noted that fact. Eight of nine is not bad. Jack was a winner on that one.

The earnings-per-share experience of the 1960s was—and Ben Graham used to write on this—that if you issued convertible preferreds and warrants nobody paid any attention until they were exercised. That was stupid, but those were the numbers that everybody was looking at it. In a rational world that would not happen, but in the real world—guys want to go out to have lunch, they want to chase girls, go to baseball games—it's an imperfect world, as Lou well knows.

WEISS: Picking up on Warren's comment, particularly about the insurance business, it strikes me that—I'm not a financial analyst and I'm not formally trained in any of these areas—but it seems to me as an observer of businesses that virtually every corporation has within its financials one or more accounts that are highly judgmental in nature. In the case of insurance it is fairly easy to identify this—how do you estimate your loss reserves. Or dealing with inventory in a retailing business. This is one of the issues that the accounting system has to deal with.

This takes us back in a different way to one of the themes of discussion over the past couple of days: How much confidence do you have in the integrity of the people who are putting out the numbers? They have to make judgments of some kind. There is no number that one can find that is the objectively right number of what your loss reserves are in your reinsurance business. There's a range of reasonableness there. It ultimately comes down to the question of trust and integrity of the managers making those estimates.

BUFFETT: What bothers me, Elliott, is that people of generally high integrity who you would trust in any situation—you could make them the trustee under your will—but it has now become the norm to feel that as a manager of a major company it is up to you to play the accounting game, particularly the ones suggested to you by your very auditor.

For example, what's happened with restructuring, what's happened with purchase accounting adjustments? I have seen significant cases where the auditors come to management and say, here is the way to do this at this point so that you can report better numbers later on. And nobody will pay attention to the numbers for this period because of this or that going on.

It is the degree to which the high grade people have either been co-opted, or acquiesced or whatever word you want to pick. And that's very tough to cleanse the system of because you don't have good guys and bad guys anymore. Six firms could get together and do it.

## Current Commentary

"The auditing profession would have done well to heed Buffett's hopeful prescriptions. Instead, as this exchange occurred in 1996, accounting frauds were underway at Enron, Global Crossing, Qwest, and WorldCom. Within a few years, when these and others were exposed, Arthur Andersen collapsed, the Sarbanes-Oxley Act restructured the auditing function, audit committees wielded newfound power over auditors, and the Public Company Accounting Oversight Board was created."

*–Larry Cunningham*

\* \* \* \* \*

*Lou Lowenstein*

*Calvin Johnson postulated that financial accounting standards are indispensable to properly functioning capital markets and stressed that the entire discipline should be dedicated to the interests of investors. While saying Buffett is usually on the side of accounting for investors, Johnson criticized Buffett's accounting for Berkshire's acquisition of Scott Fetzer as a pooling and how Berkshire accounted for inventory of World Book encyclopedias.*

LOWENSTEIN: I was quite prepared to come to Warren's defense on this but rather than accept the second or fifth best, Warren, tell me why you are so infatuated with pooling, if in fact you are.

BUFFETT: No I am not. We always use purchase accounting because, basically, that reflects the reality of the situation. In fact, I'm not sure that we ever used pooling accounting.

MUNGER: We had a partial pooling way back when.

BUFFETT: Right.

MUNGER: But basically we use purchase accounting. You're referring to the alternative computation that we make. And I think a management is entitled to tell its shareholders—and indeed should— how it looks at the substance of the situation. So, we're using the kind of accounting you'd want in our GAAP reports and we furnish alternative figures and we say, this is the kind of stuff we look at and we think they're important and this strikes us as perfectly rational.

BUFFETT: In most cases I would say the premium we pay above the net assets recorded on the books of the predecessor company overwhelmingly is for what we call economic goodwill. We don't even look at the plants. We did not look at the plants of Scott Fetzer before we bought it. We did not look at the plants of H.H. Brown before we bought it. I have not looked at the plants since—I have never seen the plants at H.H. Brown. We don't think in terms of appraising physical assets.

We think in terms of economic goodwill. We believe that economic goodwill should all be placed on the balance sheet as a purchase. We even think that if we give stock that has greater intrinsic value, that it ought to be placed on at a higher price than market price.

In terms of the inventory on World Book we use LIFO, so we are always charging current costs out—we have not had any LIFO reduction that has caused any of that to flow into income. We use current costs on a LIFO basis—obviously last in is first out and that's been reflected.

If we had our choice in accounting for Scott Fetzer—which we didn't have, first you had to allocate to certain assets the premium we paid and the residual is goodwill—we would say it's all goodwill. The plant account of Scott Fetzer on their books before purchase accounting adjustments straight through—the plant account is less now than it was when we bought the firm. So, essentially we have not been faced with the problem of the fact that the replacement value is much higher. The plant account is $49 million now—it was considerably more before, plus it makes more money.

What we were buying was economic goodwill. Fortunately, the economic goodwill has not deteriorated at Scott Fetzer. In our view, to attribute $50 million of the purchase price, let's say to plant and equipment—if someone tells us that is the replacement value—that just isn't the way we look at it. Now we may be required to put it on our books that way but we also want to tell shareholders how we look at it.

JOHNSON: Certainly the purchase method was mandatory for GAAP purposes and you did report it that way. I'll take your clarification. My criticisms were of the alternative method in which you were looking yearningly at Scott Fetzer's old asset accounts and wishing Berkshire could use them and saying they were really great.

BUFFETT: That is just the way we look at it.

JOHNSON: I agree with you that goodwill should not be depreciated. I spent a year trying to ensure that it would not be depreciated for tax purposes. I did an amicus brief for the Supreme Court and went back into Congress. And I heard from everyone that that was kind of right, that goodwill does not depreciate, it appreciates. Notwithstanding my best efforts, they allow it to be written off over fifteen years. I think that is a terrible economic decision to allow writing off over fifteen years something that we know is appreciating. I kind of wish you had joined those hearings as well as the securities hearings because maybe two Don Quixotes could have done some good.

BUFFETT: We only buy it if we think it is going to appreciate.

JOHNSON: In the twenty-first century it is going to be all goodwill. We're going to see less and less steel and more and more silicon. We're changing elements. If we don't get goodwill accounting right, then you are basically writing off the cost of corporate stock over fifteen years and that doesn't make a bit of sense.

But the remedies aren't the same. I agree with you that goodwill should be non-amortizable. But there wasn't much goodwill in the World Book acquisition so that the premium purchase price, over Scott Fetzer's books, was really all allocable to the plant and equipment accounts.

BUFFETT: We did it as required. In our view, it was all goodwill, but it was required to be broken down based on FIFO value of inventory, appraised value of property, plant and equipment, and residuals and some of it even went to deferred tax liabilities.

What we are telling shareholders is those are the rules we follow, but in our view we paid the entire premium for goodwill. We also thought that the goodwill would not depreciate in value or else we would not have bought it in the first place. And that was the way we would keep the books. But it isn't the way the books were being kept so we explained what we thought.

CUNNINGHAM: I have two questions. Lou just told us a few minutes ago that FASB in the next few years will be looking at abolishing pooling and that it would rest in peace. Calvin, do you think that is likely? My other question is with respect to depreciating goodwill: Is the issue whether it depreciates or appreciates in value or is the issue one of cost allocation?

JOHNSON: I agree with Buffett that goodwill does not ordinarily depreciate. I don't think he really means to say that World Book's factory and inventory were worthless or cost-free to him.

LOWENSTEIN: But accountants deal with it as cost allocation as we do with cost of plant and the like. And depreciation doesn't reflect the change in value but simply allocation of cost over time.

JOHNSON: Amortization of goodwill is only at 1/40—2.5% over each of forty years. So, it is depreciable, but not very depreciable. My view is that there is goodwill; goodwill is a perfectly fine concept. In the next century all companies are going to be goodwill. These software companies may have no assets—just a bunch of employees, designs, leases; they have no assets. They are worth $2 billion. It's all going to be goodwill. It is real. Nothing fake about it.

Part of it may be the poverty of the balance sheet. In theory, a balance sheet should be a wealth statement or a savings account. From a balance sheet you should be able to tell what next year's return on capital is going to be. The accountants have gone so far away from any loyalty to the balance sheet that the balance sheet is garbage. Just miscellaneous costs that have not been written off. That means that whenever anyone else buys the company they are going to have large amounts of cost greater than book value that is goodwill.

CUNNINGHAM: It sounds like this ties into your arguments about introducing present value and similar concepts into GAAP.

JOHNSON: Yes, I wish investment bankers would write the rules instead of the accountants. GAAP is real junk. GAAP is next to worthless for investors and there isn't anybody working to improve it.

MUNGER: Oh, but if you go to investment banking accounting—which exists in all the private prospectuses in the world—if you are disgusted with conventional accounting, you ought to see investment banking accounting: EBDA—earnings before deducting anything (laughter).

LOWENSTEIN: Elliott talked about GAAP being an obstacle to be overcome and others have said that in one way or another. The whole institution of FASB has come under attack and has increasingly for a number of years. Efforts to tilt the membership of FASB to a more pro-business stance, encouraged by the triumph on the stock option accounting issue, and most recently, when the FEI came forward with a proposal that would have left the agenda for FASB under external review sympathetic to the business community. I find it daunting—it certainly is inconsistent with Calvin's principle of loyalty to investors. Is anyone else troubled by this?

BUFFETT: In the 1890s there was a bill introduced in the Indiana legislature to change the value of pi to 3.2 and the legislator explained it by saying that 3.14159 was too difficult for the schoolchildren of Indiana to work with and he thought this would simplify things (laughter).[4]

---

4. Editor's Note: See Scott L. Miley, 3.1415 = Pi = Hard, *Herald Bulletin* (Anderson, IN), March 14, 2015 (noting that the proposal was based on work by an amateur mathematician, Edwin Goodwin, but was quashed by a Purdue University mathematics professor, Clarence Waldo, who disproved the postulate).

JOHNSON: I think probably for every FASB issue that management won in the last years, if the investor groups had won, that would be a grand improvement. I get a feeling that we really are going to have to throw out the FASB GAAP figures; they are so far removed from being of any help to investors. On the other hand, every company, even the ones that minimize, have to spend $300,000 a year for their accountants and there is a whole system in place. Maybe the answer is that GAAP is so corrupted by medieval theory and management influence that it's not worth it and we ought to start over again.

On the other hand, at some point, you actually have to provide information for investors. Investors can't intuit the stuff; they can't breathe it by putting their hands on a document. In the end they need accurate information analyzed in a way that makes sense within the theory of investing. The information has to fit into the model. And I don't know whether that's going to be through FASB or in spite of FASB, and I suspect it will have to be in spite of FASB.

But I also think that the country cries for it, that this is a cheap way to improve productivity in this country. If you're talking about a little genie who can move mountains with the flip of the wrist, that genie would be to get out some data that is helping investor decisions instead of helping to increase management compensation and getting them to CYA. I don't know how it's going to come out, but I do think it's important.

BUFFETT: I agree with that, but the interesting thing is we find financial information—even as presented—is enormously useful. And we have bought in the last year and a half four businesses—we're in the process of buying the fourth—where all we had was financial information plus our ability to think some about the economic characteristics. We accept—I shouldn't say we accept precisely the numbers—but the numbers as given to us from GAAP accounting are of sufficient utility to us so that we can make a judgment about buying a business without ever seeing whether a plant exists.

LOWENSTEIN: The whole hostile takeover movement in the 1980s was obviously premised on nothing more than the published financials.

BUFFETT: We do it every day. We have spent billions of dollars utilizing public financials. But there are a lot of financials we wouldn't utilize.

* * * * *

*Ed Kitch lauded The Buffett Essays for their extended narrative explanation of accounting figures, better illuminating simple measures such as earnings per share, but surmised that other corporations do not follow suit because of securities law's endorsement of GAAP and risks of liability. Buffett's response began the dialogue.*

BUFFETT: I can't recall in the last 15 years anywhere in our analysis we have actually even mentioned earnings per share. We're required to state earnings per share in the five-year summary by either the SEC or GAAP. But for the reasons you've mentioned, so much attention is paid to the figure which I think has got very, very limited use and is far less useful than looking at the results unit by unit. So I have never, that I can remember, I have never used earnings per share in the text of an annual report.

COMMENT: If you were to summarize all the problems we've been discussing over the last two days, it could fall under the category of short-term shenanigans. You can summarize the Buffett-Munger philosophy as not only a commitment to the long term, but a commitment to permanent ownership. Would a solution be if you changed the tax laws such that permanent owners would be rewarded?

Now, this has been suggested before in a number of venues. Warren once suggested a 100% capital gains tax on gains taken within one year. Others have proposed adjusting capital gains depending on how long a security was held. Warren and Charlie's example has shown the great merits of permanent investing. Perhaps all our energies could be devoted towards introducing legislation that would reward permanent or near permanent investments.

KITCH: I don't think you would necessarily have to enact legislation. It's quite clear that you can see in the organic structure of Berkshire Hathaway efforts to induce shareholders to hold. For instance, Berkshire Hathaway is quite unusual in trying to lure its shares out of street name and into registered ownership. For example, you only can take advantage of the charitable giving plan if you register your shares. The securities industry, of course, has been pushing to get rid of registered shares—let's keep everything in book accounts at the brokerage firms and so on—because, of course, it makes them easier to sell.

COMMENT: That's the specific example of Berkshire which, of course, is completely admirable. But in terms of doing something that can be done with the stroke of a pen to begin to make corporate America conform to the Berkshire mold. But as far as taking some sort of a practical first step that does something like a tax on short-term capital gains.

JIM REPETTI: That has been discussed in the past, and I think there's a problem with the assumptions. I would argue that people who are investing for their own account should always want management to be taking the long-term perspective. Because if I am investing for my own account, I know that the price I can sell this security at is going to be determined in part by the purchaser's perspective of the longer-term prospects of the company. So, you would normally expect investors to want management to take the long-term account. I have suggested in the past that the real problem is with management—the problem isn't with the investors, except for the institutional investors who may not be investing for their own account.

LOWENSTEIN: Warren made a proposal like this some years ago and then gave up on it. I've had the insensitivity, stupidity, to keep reiterating the proposal in various forms. Nancy Kassebaum, Felix Rohatyn, and

Keynes, I think, was the first to suggest a penalty for short-term trading. If you lengthen the investor's horizon you change for the better the pressures on management. As Jim said, there are a few guys down on Wall Street who probably don't quite see it that way, and judging by the flow of PAC money, they probably have a little more influence than we have.

---

**Current Commentary**

"Concern about the short-term perspective of corporate management and some money managers continues today. The tax system has proven to be ineffective in imposing a long-term perspective. Instead. we need to find better ways to align management's interests (i.e. compensation) with the long-term best interests of investors."

*—Jim Repetti*

---

FISCH: People are talking about two different things here though. The idea that we want managements to have long time-frame perspectives and you want investors to invest with the idea that they're concerned about long-term profits doesn't mean we want to preclude trading and we want to get rid of liquidity in the securities markets, and some of these proposals would threaten to do that. The whole reason people are willing to put money into the capital markets is because they offer liquidity as well as long-term profitability. And you prevent a lot of the capital that we have today from going into these forms of companies if you say you can't get your money out.

LOWENSTEIN: I would suggest that that raises the question of how much liquidity is enough and at what point the grease causes the wheels to skid and lose direction. We had 14% turnover on the big board in the year 1960, and I don't think anybody was complaining about a lack of liquidity. Now it's about 70-75% when you take the off the board trading, and where do you stop? The costs of liquidity are very, very high.

## Current Commentary

"NYSE share turnover subsequently rose to as high as 138% in 2008, before sinking back to 1996 levels in 2012 followed by an uptick thanks to frequency trading."

*—Larry Cunningham*

FISCH: Even for Berkshire Hathaway, the point of listing on the New York Stock Exchange is recognizing that investors benefit from liquidity. You want a long-term shareholder class, but you know that your investors sometimes are going to have to get out, they need to get some cash back, they need to send their kids to college or whatever.

LOWENSTEIN: I thought it was, and Warren can answer this, it was not so much the increase in the volume of trading—it looks pretty tiny still to me—but getting the dealers out of the way and getting into the true auction market. But Warren, why did you go to the big board?

BUFFETT: We didn't think the market would necessarily be more active at all. In fact, the day we listed I said to Jimmy McGuire, the specialist, "I will consider you an enormous success if the next trade in this stock is about two years from now." And they didn't seem to get enthused about that (laughter).

And anything we buy—when we buy Coca-Cola or Gillette, whatever it may be—our mindset is that we would be happy to own that security if they closed down the Exchange as they did in 1914. If we aren't happy owning a piece of that business with the Exchange closed, we're not happy owning it with the Exchange open.

Nevertheless, liquidity is a very mild plus to us. It's not a minus, it's a mild plus to Berkshire shareholders. But if it's going to be a huge plus to Berkshire holders, then we have the wrong shareholders.

**Current Commentary**

"Happily owning a stock even when the Exchange is closed speaks to Warren's belief that it is the advancement of long-term intrinsic value not short-term stock price that matters most in growing business value over time."

*—Robert Hagstrom*

LOWENSTEIN: John Maynard Keynes in *The General Theory* in that very short but very insightful chapter on investing—Chapter 12, 18 pages—had some well taken comments on liquidity, and I really recommend them to those who aren't familiar with them.

JOHNSON: We spend a lot of money in the tax law worrying about lock-in effect. We spend a lot of billions of dollars of tax giveaways in order to come in with the rough-hewn anti-lock-in remedy of capital gain preferences. Now you're telling me that we've spent 80 years wasting our money because lock-in is good instead of bad. And in a sense, we already have very intense incentives to hold onto your property. We have a step up in basis at death and we have an effective tax rate that goes down the longer that you hold onto property. That is generally conceived to be a serious problem to be overcome with capital gain preferences. Not a solution.

I also wanted to take issue with this idea that we need to have more narratives. We need numbers and a guiding North Star. A map abstracts out most facts about the land. It has none of the local character, none of the richness of the culture, none of the Gods who live in the woods except for a couple of pieces of data—North, South, East, West. On topographical maps you can find out whether you're dealing with water or sand and that's about it. That's what makes maps so comparable.

I have to work very hard to teach my students that financial analysts abstract the investment to such a degree that we don't even know whether it's a gumball machine or a widget factory or annuity underneath. We are, in fact, trying to get data out of this in order to abstract it. I think life in all its fullness provides no answer to any riddle, it's just an absolute incomprehensible mush of junk. When you finally come up with figures, then you finally get something that's worthwhile.

MUNGER: I think you understand the mush better if you look at it from two or three viewpoints. Take a building. If you look at it from the top and the side and maybe an architect's plan, you understand the building much better than if you just have one view. So, I'm afraid that reality is messy. And if you want to understand it you've got to be able to handle the whole mess. Einstein said, "Everything should be made as simple as possible, but no more so."

\* \* \* \* \*

*Jim Repetti gave a comprehensive review of corporate tax laws, especially those involving management and shareholder relationships, such as golden parachutes, repudiating those that subsidize managerial inefficiency, such as the capital gains preference and differential corporate versus individual tax rates.*

LOWENSTEIN: Does that mean you would like to see elimination of the corporate tax as is sometimes proposed?

REPETTI: One of the proposals that has been made to change the tilt in the playing field has been to eliminate the tax on dividends—that is, to retain the tax on corporate income at the corporate level, but eliminate the tax on the distributions of those earnings to stockholders. That would certainly put a lot more pressure on management, maybe too much pressure. That would be tilting the playing field in the other direction.

I also think that there may be some revenue concerns. Even though the corporate tax only accounts for about 12% now of our total federal receipts, that would be a 12% shortfall that we would create if we eliminated the corporate tax. I don't want to tilt the field one way or the other, I just want a level playing field.

---

**Current Commentary**

"In 2003, the tax rate for capital gains and dividends became equal. Economists cannot agree whether this parity affected corporate dividend policy."

*—Jim Repetti*

---

MUNGER: I think there are absolutely dispositive answers to some of these questions. If you're going to run a democracy, you've got to have some general regard for the law which at least is not horribly resentful.

The guy who has $5 million in dividend income, pays no income tax. Yet a taxi driver working 90 hours a week is paying 30 or 40% of the income in taxes.

It's so unendurable that any program that contemplates it, whatever its theoretical merits, is a non-starter. So, I just don't think you could even consider that kind of an answer. The system has to pay some attention to egalitarian instincts.

REPETTI: You mean eliminating the tax on dividend income. You think it's just politically impossible?

LOWENSTEIN: The alternative that might bridge those two, of course, is one that sometimes discusses eliminating the corporate tax and having a flow-through tax of corporate earnings taxed to the shareholders.

MUNGER: I would argue on the other hand that we want to live in a civilization—so long as we've got private capitalism—with substantial accumulations of corporate earnings. That is the great engine of the future growth of the economic pie, and it's much simpler and surer to be there if the people that earn it just keep it. And so I think you want a civilization where the incentives in place leave at least half of what corporate America earns on its stock routinely accumulated.

REPETTI: I think your company has the best solution, regardless of how we change the tax—the law; your returns are so great that stockholders would normally elect to—

MUNGER: It would be a huge mistake to assume that Berkshire Hathaway is the right model for all America. It would be an absolute disaster if every single corporation in America suddenly tried to turn itself into a clone of Berkshire Hathaway.

LOWENSTEIN: Charlie likes to say half of the world is below average, and for the companies who are happily year after year earning 8% on shareholders' capital, Berkshire Hathaway is not the one.

BUFFETT: We would follow the same dividend policy if we were owned 100% by a tax-free institution. But that's not necessarily the case generally in corporate America.

---

### Current Commentary

"President Obama's proposed 2016 budget estimated that corporate taxes would constitute 13.4% of total tax revenues that year. Yet concern has grown about the impact of a U.S. system that defers U.S. tax on profits of foreign subsidiaries until the earnings are repatriated. Many worry that U.S. multinationals simply keep profits offshore to avoid U.S. tax. Debate rages as to whether the U.S. should give up trying to tax foreign earnings by adopting a 'territorial tax' or instead end the deferral of U.S. tax on earnings of foreign subsidiaries. In addition, low corporate tax rates in other counties create pressure on the U.S. to lower its corporate tax rate as a 'race to the bottom' is developing."

*—Jim Repetti*

---

JOHNSON: I think that golden parachutes legislation was another example of Congress fighting in favor of local industry and entrenched management. I know that in form this was a penalty on extraordinary severance paid to the target management, and it sounds like it's a penalty on the target and on something that's pro-target instead of pro-shark. But I think that the understood motive apart from the political rhetoric of it was, in fact, to get rid of an extraordinarily useful pro-shark technique.

REPETTI: I like golden parachute payments if they're approved by the stockholders after full disclosure to the stockholders of the facts. If you start with a model where you have a separation of ownership from control, you have to assume that some of the bidding companies are themselves not seeking to maximize profits but are trying to achieve other objectives that may be harmful to the stockholders of the target company in the long term. And in that sort of situation it may make sense to try to allow management to entrench itself. Again, I believe in corporate democracy. I think if the stockholders, after they've been told what is good for them or what's not good for them, after they've spoken then let the chips fall where they may.

MUNGER: How do you feel about what I regard as by far the most important of the tax provisions that deterred takeovers—in terms of practical importance I think it dwarfs all the others. That's when Congress repealed the *General Utilities* doctrine.[5] That really changed the arithmetic of takeovers in a way that discouraged takeovers. If you want to write-off the assets and get future tax benefits, the existing C corporation is going to have to pay a huge tax at its level. That was profoundly an anti-takeover provision. Are you for it or against it?

REPETTI: I was in favor of that because it seemed to me that balancing against any concerns you may have had about the takeover market, that it made sense from a tax policy perspective that it was consistent with the way we were treating other corporate transactions outside the purchase situation. For example, when a corporation distributes an appreciated asset to a stockholder, that triggers a tax at the corporate level as well as at the stockholder level.

MUNGER: They changed that at the same time.

---

5. Editor's Note: The reference is to a 1935 U.S. Supreme Court case, General Utilities Co. v. Helvering, 296 U.S. 200 (1935), holding that corporations recognize no gain or loss when they distribute appreciated property to stockholders, subject to varying exceptions and limitations courts developed over the decades. All of that, dubbed the General Utilities Doctrine and seen generally to encourage corporate acquisitions, was repealed in the Tax Reform Act of 1986, so that corporations generally do recognize gain or loss on most distributions of appreciated property to stockholders. Exceptions remain for liquidations and spin-offs of controlled subsidiaries.

REPETTI: Right.

MUNGER: How about you, Cal?

JOHNSON: This is an extraordinarily interesting story, because most of the academics love it and say that it came out of the American Law Institute. The American Law Institute has a good government tradition going back to the 1930s. It really looked like it came out of the academy. When in 1986 Congress passed this, all the pointy-headed academics were taking credit for it, celebrating that finally Congress is paying attention to the American Law Institute.

The reality of it is that Congress passed *General Utilities* repeal in 1986 to prevent takeovers. It was a way to penalize those managements that did want to sell out to Wall Street. It's just another indication that Congress is very much in favor of Main Street as against Wall Street.

MUNGER: How would you have voted on the change if you were in Congress?

JOHNSON: I've got another difficulty, and that is at my heart I'm a tax man, and my first loyalty is to get the tax system right. Jim and I are in agreement on repeal of *General Utilities* being right. I'm not doing your business. My loyalty is to the state of the tax system.

---

### Current Commentary

"Corporations still struggle with the impact of the repeal of *General Utilities*. Yahoo's ill-fated attempt to spin off its valuable Alibaba stock in 2015 was motivated by the tax impact of the repeal of *General Utilities*."

—*Jim Repetti*

---

*Charlie Munger, Elliott Weiss*

**Current Commentary**

"I now think Buffett's greatest accomplishment is building a giant conglomerate while successfully projecting a public image of a down-to-earth, folksy, regular guy persona. Buffett's whole approach to public relations and regulatory affairs has been quite different from the usual practice. He does the most important part himself. He goes and talks to regulatory personnel face-to-face. The Omaha location helps, and the county-fair style shareholder meetings help. And indeed, his willingness to participate in this event was part of this approach."

*—Ed Kitch*

# REMINISCENCES

WE HAD A WONDERFUL SYMPOSIUM AND THE whole weekend was a treat. You get a sense of the intellectual discourse as well as the good humor from this transcript. The many off-the-record occasions enriched the gathering as well, including during meals, breaks, and informal outings.

After corresponding with Warren for many months in planning the symposium, I first met him in person that weekend when I hosted a dinner for all guests at Il Cantinori, an Italian restaurant in Greenwich Village. When I introduced myself by name and extended my hand, he said, "Oh, nice to meet you, you are the fellow who rearranged my letters."

After dinner, a group of us professors went out for drinks along with Charlie, at the Temple Bar in the East Village—where people's heads turned. The next morning, when we reported that to Warren, he joked: "If people recognized Charlie, it must have been a gay bar." Meanwhile, earlier at breakfast, Dale Oesterle sat with Munger, and for the longest time, did not know who he was.

Walking to the conference later with Munger, he told me he was trying to determine why Buffett had agreed to let me rearrange and publish his letters, as I apparently was not the first person to conceive of such an idea. We surmised, however, that it was due to trust-based relationships: my colleague and former Dean Monroe Price contacted one of Warren's best friends, Bob Denham, who presented the proposal for me. I also enlisted help from my friend and former boss at Cravath, Swaine & Moore, Sam Butler, whom Warren had known for decades—he was on GEICO's board when Berkshire bought its first stake.

Another mutual friend is Cravath partner, George Gillespie, Warren's personal estate lawyer and fellow director for years on the board of Washington Post Co. To the symposium George carried with him an updated version of Warren's will for signing. When George asked me for a room where Warren could do so—and for me to be a witness—Warren quipped: "If you're going to be a witness, then I guess you're not in it."

We put Munger up, along with the professors, at The Gramercy Park Hotel, then an old family business whose luster had dimmed—years later it was renovated into a world class hotel. Munger described the hotel as "totally adequate." The second night, Samuel and Ronnie Heyman hosted a dinner for our guests and friends of the University. I left with Munger and took a cab back to Gramercy. After we hopped in, Munger leaned back and sighed: "I've never been in a room with so much money gathered in it."

During the conference the next day, my nephew Justin got to meet Warren. Justin was only a 13-year-old so didn't know exactly who Warren was, saying he signified "lots of zeroes."

Years later, Bill Ackman reminded me that this is when he first met Warren. Apparently, in line at the lunch buffet, Bill began chatting with Warren's wife Susan. The two seemed to hit it off, with Susan, one of the most gracious ladies I've known, inviting Bill to sit at her table.

It was Jeff Gordon who had the idea to offer Berkshire-themed products at the symposium. Besides serving Coke and See's peanut brittle, we distributed copies of *The Washington Post* both days. In a salute to Salomon, we followed investment banking practice of memorializing important transactions with a "deal toy"—such as a miniature prospectus inside a Lucite cube. We put the symposium program inside one of those for all participants. A week later, Debbie Bosanek, Warren's assistant, told me he cheerfully brought it into his office to use as a paperweight—so I sent her one too.

My student assistants and I had coordinated many logistical details for the weekend, but after the symposium ended on Monday, we realized we had not made arrangements to get the Buffett family (Warren, Susan, and Howard) to the airport. They said they would simply get a taxi and the three of them, with luggage, ambled out to Fifth Avenue in Manhattan near rush hour to hail one.

I insisted that we could easily get them a town car for the trip but Warren declined saying the cab would be cheaper. I said we'd spring for it and wouldn't tell anyone about the indulgence. Howard quickly intoned: "But I'll tell." They all got in the cab. Ever since, I've always thought, Howard will make a good chairman of the Berkshire board someday.

L.A.C.

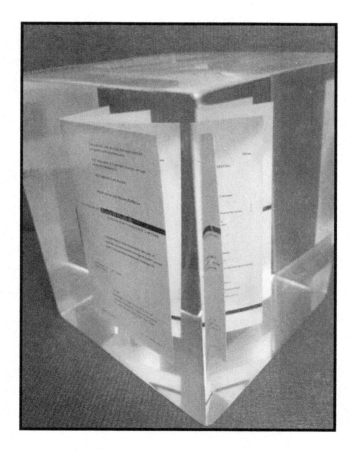

*Lucite Cube with Symposium Program*

# GALLERY

*Peter Hilal, Warren Buffett, Paul Hilal, Charlie Munger*

*Charlie Munger, Bill Ackman, Chris Stavrou*

*Warren Buffett, Justin Cunningham, Larry Cunningham*

*Larry Cunningham, George Gillespie*

*George Gillespie, Howard Buffett, Ajit Jain*

*Ajit Jain, Susan and Warren Buffett, Charlie Munger*

*Marjorie Knowles, Susan Buffett, Deborah DeMott*

*Leah Spiro, Charlie Munger*

# SUBSEQUENT STEPS

THE YEAR AFTER THE SYMPOSIUM, WE PUBLISHED *THE Essays of Warren Buffett: Lessons for Corporate America* as a stand-alone publication carved out of the symposium volume. We offered it at Berkshire's 1998 annual meeting, at Borsheim's on Sunday, thanks to CEO Susan Jacques.

Below are some photos of me and my team, including my nephew Justin and my research assistant, Dana Auslander, later a successful hedge fund executive, setting up and selling. As you can see, we had our own kiosk and *The Essays* was the only book offered for sale.

*Larry Cunningham, Matt McMerdo, Justin Cunningham,
Dana Auslander, Annie Rusher*

Below is a picture of Warren when he returned to my school a few years later to teach one of my classes. At front left is my student, Andrew Sole, who went on to become a successful value investor.

Press interest in *The Essays,* including the symposium, has always been strong, though it grew considerably over the years. Among earliest treatments was a 1998 interview in *Forbes,* reprinted below, followed by a kind note from Warren referencing it. The date of the letter is earlier than that of the magazine due to that old tradition of print magazines being issued ahead of their print date in order to extend their shelf life! Copies would also be sent to subscribers immediately on publication.

---

Warren Buffett says he doesn't think the market is overvalued, yet he buys few stocks. Why?

# Three little words

By Subrata N. Chakravarty

NOT ONLY DO INVESTORS hang on Warren Buffett's every word, they spend countless hours trying to read between the lines. Over the past three years Lawrence A. Cunningham, 35, a professor at Yeshiva University's Cardozo School of Law in New York City, has gone one step further: He has compiled and distilled 20 years of Buffett's annual letters to Berkshire Hathaway shareholders. The result: *The Essays of Warren Buffett: Lessons for Corporate America* (Cardozo Law Review, $14.95). Buffett himself called the book a "superb job." Here, Cunningham tells why he went to the effort.

Cardozo law school's Lawrence Cunningham; Berkshire Hathaway's Warren Buffett.
**The song he sings was written by Ben Graham.**

**FORBES: Why is a law professor interested in the letters of Warren Buffett?**
I'm a corporate governance scholar. There's an intersection between law and government [which is] where I write and teach. Buffett's essays are full of profound wisdom on governance and related themes.
**Most chief executives brush the owners off with a few clichés. Why does Buffett go to all this trouble?**
The reason is precisely that he would want this kind of letter written to him. He wants the people who have entrusted their wealth to him to know how he thinks about allocating their capital. He wants them to understand what his choices and tradeoffs are and how he goes about choosing among them.
**Why did you, an academic, put this collection together?**

I'd like to have finance professors teach students about fundamental valuation analysis again, rather than about modern finance theory. [Modern finance theory teaches] that you're better off throwing darts rather than spending time thinking about whether investment opportunities make business sense.
Efficient market theorists tell you that price is the same as value. Buffett thinks markets are somewhat efficient but not perfect. He quotes Ben[jamin] Graham [Buffett's teacher and mentor] on that point: That in the short run stock markets are voting machines; in the long run they're weighing machines.
On a daily basis, Graham taught, people are expressing hopes and fears. But over a long period of time, the voting will be corrected and the gap

between price and value will narrow. We've had a bull market for 15 years. This isn't Ben Graham's world, is it?
Graham would say we're just experiencing a phase where there is an extraordinary amount of greed, and a mind-set of endless prosperity. What Graham wouldn't understand—what would be totally unrecognizable to him—is the degree to which fashionable academics think that these emotions have been purged from the market process, that the market is getting it right every day and that price and value are functionally identical.
**You went through 20 years of Buffett's essays. Has his thinking changed?**
Very, very little. There are a couple of examples of evolution, but it's quite incremental and the foundation is permanent. It's fundamental valuation analysis.
**I doubt Ben Graham would have bought and held stocks like Coca-Cola that sell for more than 40 times earnings and a huge premium to book value.**
Graham was very rigid in thinking about value and value investing in his approach. Over time, in part with the guidance and goading of [Berkshire Hathaway Vice Chairman] Charlie Munger, Buffett has accepted harder-to-measure meanings of value, like management integrity and ownership orientation, product strength and brand recognition, which are harder to quantify.
Munger is a high-powered brain. They help each other—a productive dialogue that stimulates thought and learning—but with the same core philosophical base.
**Insisting as he does on value, Buffett has almost no tech stocks.**
Buffett quotes [IBM founder] Thomas Watson: "I'm only smart in spots—but I stay around those spots." Buffett defines his circle of competence pretty narrowly. He admires and respects [Intel's] Andy Grove and [Microsoft's] Bill Gates, but he says he doesn't understand their products well enough to form a

valuation judgment.
**Buffett criticizes the practice of granting huge stock options to managements. But isn't this a way to align management interests with those of shareholders?**
Options are very different from ownership. The manager becomes an owner if things go well, but if things go badly, he or she suffers not at all. A second criticism is that option granting tends to be unrelated to real business performance.
At Berkshire, they pay bonuses in cash, based on performance of areas under managerial control.
Buffett is scathing on the measurement of Earnings Before Interest, Taxes and Depreciation [EBITD], calling it "an abomination."
[He recognizes that] depreciation is a real economic cost. So when you say: "Let's just look at the cash flows," you're ignoring an important part of the cost of maintaining your competitive position. EBITD was, in part, a way to approve loans that did not make good economic sense.
Another Buffett peeve is zero coupon bonds.
In the beginning they made sense as a way to lock in a return. The trouble is it becomes easy for weaker credits to load up on debt. That's why he says of zeroes: "What the wise do in the beginning, fools do in the end."
**What's it tell us, that he bought zero Treasurys and silver?**
That it's hard to find equity investments where there is a margin of safety these days, [but] it's a mistake to wonder why Buffett did this or that. People should concentrate on the core principles of fundamental analysis. Graham's most profound investment insight was the "margin of safety" principle, which said: Never buy a security unless the price is substantially lower than the value.
**I guess this explains why he *isn't* buying many new stocks, even though he doesn't think the market overall is overvalued. He just can't find that margin of safety.**
Graham said that the three words that are key to investment success are "margin of safety." Buffett still thinks those are the right three words. ∎

Forbes *article, April 6, 1998*

BERKSHIRE HATHAWAY INC.
1440 KIEWIT PLAZA
OMAHA, NEBRASKA 68131
TELEPHONE (402) 346·1400

WARREN E. BUFFETT, CHAIRMAN

March 23, 1998

Via Facsimile #212-790-0205

Lawrence A. Cunningham
Professor of Law & Director
Heyman Center on Corporate Governance
Benjamin N. Cardozo School of Law
Yeshiva University
Brookdale Center
55 Fifth Avenue
New York, NY 10003-4391

Dear Larry:

Thanks for the nice words in *Forbes* — you say it better than I do.

Best regards.

Sincerely,

Warren E. Buffett

*Letter from Warren Buffett, March 23, 1998*

Subsequent to the original 1997 edition, *The Essays of Warren Buffett: Lessons for Corporate America* was published in new editions in 2001, 2007, 2013, and 2015. Cover images follow.

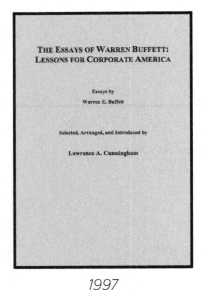

*1997*

*2001*

*2007*

*2013*

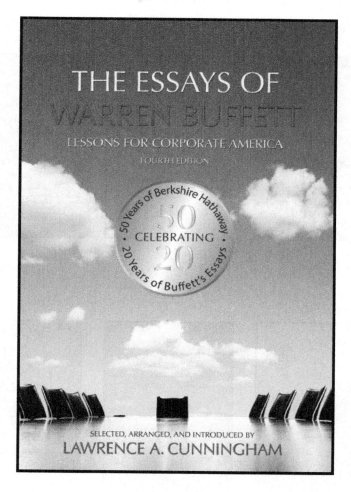

*2015*

Thanks to Warren's encouragement, starting with an inquiry he received from China, I arranged for the translation of *The Essays* into Chinese, French, German, Greek, Japanese, Korean, Portuguese, Russian, Spanish, Thai, and Vietnamese. Selected cover images below.

Chinese

French

Japanese

Korean

Spanish

Thai

When we first sold *The Essays* at the 1998 Berkshire annual meeting, it was the only book offered there. By 2015, The Bookworm, an Omaha bookstore, had its own exhibit at the Berkshire meeting, where it offers for sale some forty titles, all handpicked by Warren. Besides *The Essays*, I was honored that another of my books was included, *Berkshire Beyond Buffett: The Enduring Value of Values*. Below is a photo where I stood at the Bookworm exhibit during the lunch break autographing in 2015. The Hudson Bookstore in Omaha is also a big seller of books concerning Buffett and Berkshire, including my books.

# NOTES FROM OMAHA

I F YOU'VE NEVER ATTENDED A BERKSHIRE ANNUAL meeting, go. A big draw remains Warren and Charlie's Saturday Q&A with shareholders, now live-streamed on the internet. The Q&A explores diverse topics, but attend multiple meetings and you'll discover that everything turns on a few fundamentals. The day after my fifth meeting, Charlie Munger summed it up to me: "So you got another dose of the catechism."

Yet if Berkshire Saturday is like going to church, the rest of the weekend feels like a festive family reunion. Make new friends and catch up with old ones during the many professional and social gatherings studding the weekend. Here are my highlights from the annual pilgrimage:

1. *Talks*: U. Nebraska/Bob Miles Summit (Thursday); Creighton U. Roundtable (Friday).

2. *Events*: Andy & Pat Kilpatrick's party; Whitney Tilson's reception.

3. *Spectacle*: Scores of Berkshire subsidiaries selling wares at discounts in the arena's vast exhibition hall.

4. *Scene*: Berkshire CEOs strolling the lobby of the Hilton as Liz Claman broadcasts.

5. *Outings*: Minor League Baseball (Friday night); Borsheim's (Sunday afternoon).

6. *Restaurant*: V. Merz (every year when paying our check, we reserve for the next year).

7. *People*: Meeting my loyal readers from Oklahoma to India!

8. *Personal moment*: Op-ed in the *Omaha World Herald* meeting edition.

9. *Book distribution method*: John Petry and Joel Greenblatt bought 5000 copies of *The Essays* after founding Value Investors Club in 2001, distributed free from the back of a U-Haul truck parked outside the meeting hall entrance.

10. *Family*: Sharing the weekend year after year with my wife Stephanie!

# EPILOGUE

A LOT CHANGED AT BERKSHIRE FROM 1996 TO 2016, especially a vast multiplication in size from a company comprised mainly of minority common stock positions to a conglomerate boasting scores of wholly-owned businesses—ten so large that they would qualify as Fortune 500 companies standing alone.

|  | 1996 | 2016 |
|---|---|---|
| Book value per share | $20,000 | $150,000 |
| Class A share price | $35,000 | $200,000 |
| Market capitalization | $60 | $320 |
| Book value of marketable securities | $30 | $120 |
| Book value of operating assets | $2 | $500 |
| Net earnings | $2.5 | $20 |
| Wholly-owned direct subsidiaries | 15 | 60 |
| Acquisition cost of direct subsidiaries | <$5 | >$170 |
| Shareholders' equity | $25 | $250 |
| Float | $7 | $85 |
| Directors | 6 | 12 |
| Employees | 33,000 | 350,000 |
| Employees at headquarters | 12 | 25 |
| Annual meeting attendance | 7,000 | 40,000 |

*Berkshire: 1996 v. 2016*

*Dollars in billions except per share amounts. Many figures are averaged or rounded for salience.*

Berkshire has generated enormous excess cash over the past two decades that Buffett and Munger deployed to build a corporate fortress. Its strength derives from how Berkshire finances operations and acquisitions: primarily through retained earnings, with leverage contributed by insurance float and deferred taxes.

Berkshire generally does not use banks or other intermediaries. In the few cases where Berkshire has borrowed funds, mostly for use of its capital intensive and regulated public utility and railroad business, loans are long-term and fixed-rate. Use of traditional debt could juice Berkshire's results, but borrowed money is also costly and creates risk of default along with collateral damage.

When insurance underwriting is done with discipline over long periods of time, the amount of float can grow to large proportions. At Berkshire, float rose from a mere $7 billion in 1996 to $84 billion in 2016. Thanks to its long holding periods, Berkshire's deferred taxes have accumulated to nearly $58 billion today, making the total of these unconventional leverage sources $142 billion.

Unlike float (or deferred taxes), bank debt comes with covenants, stated interest, and due dates. And loans are marketed by an agent whose interests conflict with those of borrowers, whether concerning a loan's size, duration, cost, or covenants. Berkshire's self-reliance provides the leverage benefits of debt (more assets deployed) without the costs, constraints, and conflicts.

The other great example of Berkshire's self-reliance concerns acquisitions. Whereas most corporations use a strategic plan to scout for and vet targets, Berkshire awaits possibilities, rejects most that are presented, and seizes on the attractive ones opportunistically. It publishes strict acquisition criteria for all to see, including a requirement that offers include a price—and there is rarely any haggling over price in a Berkshire acquisition.

Similarly, in typical acquisitions, as negotiations of the terms of agreement proceed, accountants test a company's controls and financial figures while lawyers probe contracts, compliance, and litigation. Such examinations are usually done at corporate headquarters, along with meetings where principals get acquainted and tour facilities. The process can take months and generate significant fees. Berkshire—proudly—does little of that.

Buffett sizes people up in minutes; deals are sometimes reached in an initial phone call, often in meetings of less than two hours and invariably within a week. Formal contracts are completed promptly. Deals—including those involving billions of dollars—can close within a month of the initial contact. The process does not reflect lack of information but rather Buffett's and Munger's prodigious business reading, which has yielded broad knowledge and familiarity with many companies.

Moreover, they have disciplined themselves to stick with areas of expertise, so if they lack understanding they know it and pass. It is not an accident that Berkshire hasn't purchased a high-tech business. To paraphrase Robert Hagstrom's thoughtful current commentary for this annotated transcript, beware your cognitive defects. And to paraphrase Charlie from the symposium, be afraid of your own idiocy.

Many people are interested in replicating Berkshire Hathaway, from the current leadership of Google to smaller insurance companies such as Markel Corporation, which has consciously mimicked the model quite successfully on a lesser scale. Many Berkshire subsidiaries are themselves conglomerates, genuine mini-Berkshires including not only Marmon Group and Scott Fetzer but Berkshire Hathaway Energy, MiTek, and Precision Cast Parts.

Business people dream of creating conglomerates in Berkshire's image in much the same way proverbial literary types want to write the next best-selling novel. And it can be done, if not on the same scale or to the same degree. More modest aspirations would emulate some of Berkshire's principles and practices, especially those of self-reliance as well as autonomy, decentralization, permanence, and trust.

Adapting the Berkshire model can create a competitive advantage versus rivals in the acquisition market, from strategic buyers to private equity firms. GE, for example, cannot offer autonomy or permanence. It is very acquisitive, but nearly as prone to divestitures—former CEO Jack Welch became famous for closing or selling any subsidiary that failed to lead its industry and his successor, Jeff Immelt, executed a significant divestiture program at GE. Private equity firms are interventionist by strategy and short term by design. They create funds with ten-year lives (five to sow, then five to reap) and immediately alter target managers, cultures, workforces and production facilities to prepare the company for resale.

If nothing else, every public company should learn from Berkshire the value of a long-term outlook. When public company managers are hounded by edgy analysts and certain activist shareholders about results in the current quarter and year-to-date, the pressure to focus on the short-term is intense. Cutting costs today and maximizing revenue now easily entail a sacrifice in future economic gain.

Despite Berkshire's outsize growth over the past two decades, Buffett's philosophy remained firm. If we held another such symposium today, we would include all the same panels and discussion would closely resemble that of the original. We would add panels to discuss Berkshire's scale along with its peculiar system of governance, approach to acquisitions, and deep decentralization. We would have panels featuring Berkshire subsidiaries and their managers to discuss their operations as well as Berkshire culture.

The symposium would span four days instead of two; we would serve not only Coca-Cola and See's but also Dairy Queen and anything that might require Heinz condiments. Given that Berkshire today is a microcosm of corporate America, the variety of mementos we could offer goes well beyond Lucite deal toys, and might include apparel, jewelry, or party favors. If the same people participated again, one constant you can count on is a considerable dose of wit and wisdom.

# INDEX

accounting
  discretion, 58
  information, utility of, 66
  inventories, 61-64
  judgments, 58-60
  mergers, 58, 61, 62, 64
Ackman, William, xi, xxi, xxv, 3, 30, 35, 36, 80, 83
advisory board, xii
American Law Institute, 16, 76
antitrust, 9, 46, 51
Arthur Andersen, 58, 59, 61
auctions, 5, 38, 39, 47, 49, 55, 70
auditing profession, 10, 11, 58, 60, 61
Auslander, Dana, 87, 88

Bank of America, 32
Benjamin Moore, 14
*Berkshire Beyond Buffett: The Enduring Value of Values*, 95
Berkshire Hathaway
  1996 v. 2016 data, 97
  annual meeting, xx, 77, 87, 95
  board characteristics, xii-xiii
  board meetings, xiii-vix
  charitable giving plan, 24, 68
  Class A and Class B shares, xvi, 33
  dividend policy, 26-27
  dividend policy and tax issues, 23-27
  listing on NYSE, 74
  partnership attitude, x, 20
  recapitalization, xvi
  returns, 78

shareholder polls on divided policy, 23-28
shareholder tax basis, xii, 54
Berkowitz, Bruce, xi, 3
Bevelin, Peter, ix, xxi
Bill and Melinda Gates Foundation, xiii
Bilodeau, Otis, xi
biology, 58
board roles
  crisis intervention, 8
  managerial selection, 13-15
  review of CEO, 13-14
  takeovers, 15, 41-47
Borsheim's, 87
Bratton, William, xxv, 23-24, 29
Buffett, Howard, xi, xiv, xxiii, xxiv, 13, 80, 81, 85
Buffett, Susan, xi, xxii, xxiv, 3, 80, 85, 86
Buffett Partnership, ix
Buffett, Warren, passim
Buffett questions
  dividend polls, 24
  modern finance theory, 31
  takeover decision making, 43-45
Buffett quips
  on contingent fees, 53
  on death, 34
  on mediocre managers, 6, 14
  on non-exit strategy, 19
  on partnership attitude, 20
  on redefining pi, 65
  on stock exchange closure, 70
  on strategic plans, 16

Buffett tutorials
  accounting discretion, 58
  capital allocation, 6
  earnings manipulation, 60
  earnings per share, 67
  economic goodwill, 62-63
  embarrassment, 6, 15
  first class managers, 13-15
  focused investing, 17, 19
  intrinsic value, 47
  negotiated value, 47
  subsidiary dividend policy, 25
Burger King, xix
Butler, Samuel, 79

CalPERS, 36
capital allocation, 6, 35
Cardozo, xxi, 1
Chase-Chemical merger, 46-47
Coca-Cola, xx, 31, 70, 80, 100
cognitive biases or defects, 35, 37, 99
conglomerates, x, xvi, xvii, xix, 77, 97, 99
controlling shareholders, xii, 20,
Coopers & Lybrand, 58
corporate concentrations, 12
corporate governance
  boards, 8, 13-15, 41-47
  corporate culture, xii, xiv, xvii, xviii,
    11, 16, 48, 52, 100
  corporate democracy, 5, 75
  internal control, xii, 7, 10, 11
  shareholders, 41-43
corporate tax, xix, 72-74
cosmetic accounting, 58
Cox, Jim, 41
Cravath, Swaine & Moore, 79, 80
Cunningham, Justin, 80, 84
Cunningham, Lawrence, passim

debt, x, 27, 48, 52, 59, 98
Decker, Susan, xiv
deferred tax liabilities, 27, 64, 98
Delaware corporate law, 42, 52, 53, 55
Denham, Robert, xi, xxv, 3, 4, 79

DeMott, Deborah, xxi, xxv, 17, 20, 51,
  86
Dodd-Frank Act, xii
disclosure practice and policy, xi, xix, 23,
  33-34, 75
dividend policy
  in general, 23-27
  of Berkshire, 26-27
  of Berkshire subsidiaries, 25-26
Du Pont Company, 19

earnings per share, 59, 67
economic goodwill, 62-63
Einstein, Albert, xi, 72
Eisenberg, Melvin, xxv, 7, 9, 10, 11
embarrassment, 6, 12, 15
Enron, 61
*The Essays of Warren Buffett: Lessons for
  Corporate America*, ix, x, 1, 29, 87,
  92, 93
executive compensation, 17
exit strategy, 19

Farnam Street, 26
Fechheimer Brothers, 14
fiduciary duty, xv, 17, 20
FIFO, 64
Financial Accounting Standards Board,
  64, 65, 66
Financial Executives Institute, 65
Fisch, Jill, xxv, 7, 8, 10, 11, 46, 69, 70
float, 27, 97, 98
focused investing (aka focus investing),
  17, 19
Forbes, 90-91
Foreign Corrupt Practices Act, xii

GAAP, xix, 62, 63, 65, 66, 67
Gates, Bill, xiii
General Electric, 32
General Motors, 15, 19
General Utilities doctrine, 75-76
Gillespie, George, xi, xxii, 80, 84, 85
Gillette Company, xvii, 31, 70
Global Crossing, 61

golden parachutes, 72, 74, 75
Goldman Sachs, 32
goodwill, 62-65
Gordon, Jeffrey, xxi, xxv, 11, 36, 39, 41, 43-50, 53-55, 80
Gottesman, Sandy, xi, xiii, xxi, xii, xxiii, 21
Gramercy Park Hotel, 80

Hagstrom, Robert, xxi, xxv, 19, 31, 37, 40, 71, 99
Hamilton, Robert, xxv, 23, 33, 34
Hart-Scott-Rodino, 46
Heyman, Sam & Ronnie, xxi, 2, 80
Hilal, Paul, xi, xxi, xxv, 3, 5, 12, 83
Hilal, Peter, 4, 83
H.H. Brown, 62
Holdcroft, James, xxv, 3, 4
hostile takeovers, xvii, 42, 48, 49, 52, 66
Hughes, Mark, xxi, 27

Icahn, Carl, xvii
income inequality, xix, 73
index investing, 9, 35, 36
institutional investors, xv, 7-9, 68
integrity, 60
internal auditing, xviii, 11
internal control, xii, 7, 10, 11
intrinsic value, 25, 45, 47, 48, 62, 71
inventory accounting, 61-64
inversions, xix
investing
    focused, 17-19
    indexed, 9, 35, 36
    relational, 17-19

Jacobs, Jack, xi
Jacques, Susan, 87
Jain, Ajit, xi, xxii, xxiii, 85
Johnson, Calvin, xxv, 57, 61, 63-66, 71, 74, 76
Johns Manville, 14

Kassebaum, Nancy, 68
Keynes, John Maynard, 69, 71

Kitch, Edmund, xxi, xxv, 20, 28-30, 57, 67, 68, 77
Kohlberg Kravis Roberts (KKR), xvii
Knowles, Marjorie, xi, xxv, 7, 9, 15

Lafayette Investments, 27
Larson Juhl, 14
laughter (at symposium), xxi, 5, 8, 9, 10, 13, 17, 18, 20, 24-30, 34, 46, 47, 51, 53-56, 58, 65, 70
legal education, 29
legal requirements v. good practice, 33-34
leveraged acquisitions, 48, 52
LIFO, 59, 62
liquidity, xvi, 69-71
long-term, 8, 19, 28, 36, 52, 67, 68-71, 75, 98, 100
Loomis, Carol, xi, xxii, xxiii
Lorsch, Jay, 8
Lowenstein, Louis, xi, xxv, 57, 59, 61, 64-66, 68-74
Lowenstein, Roger, xi
Lubrizol, 14

Macey, Jonathan, xxv, 3-5, 7, 12
Macey-Holdcroft proposal, 7, 12
McGuire, Jimmy, 70
McMerdo, Matt, 88
media pressure, 6
mediocre manager, 6, 14
merger accounting, 58-64
Millstein, Ira, ix, xi, xiii, xxv, 3, 6, 8-11, 16, 21
modern finance theory, ix, xv, 28, 31
Mundheim, Robert, xi, xxv, 4, 6
Munger, Charles, passim
Munger questions
    General Utilities doctrine, 75-76
    high-beta investing, 28-29
    horizontal combinations, 50
    social proof, 38
Munger quips
    on Berkshire clones, 74
    on "closet indexing", 36

on cynicism, 51
on EBITDA (or EBDA), 65
on idiocy, 39
on "investment banker" accounting, 65
on "no-talk" merger agreements, 56
on "to a man with a hammer", 35
on trivia, 30
on "whose bread I eat", 53
Munger tutorials
  concentrations of power, 12
  "experts" in takeovers, 53
  "jerk" acquirers, 20-21
  income inequality, 73
  mental models, 30, 40
  minimum standards, 33-34
  monkey experiments, 58
  multidisciplinary models, 38-39, 40, 72
  opportunity cost, 25
  second-order consequences, 12, 55
  self-criticism, 51
  trivial knowledge, 29-30

Nat'l Assn. Corporate Directors, xi, 10
National Student Marketing, 59
negotiated value, 42, 47
NetJets, 14
New York Stock Exchange, 16, 70
non-exit strategy, 19

Oesterle, Dale, xxi, xxv, 36, 41, 48-52, 79
Olson, Ron, xiii
opportunity cost, 25-26
Organizational Sentencing Guidelines, xii
owner-related business principles, xii

Pampered Chef, 14
Parrish, Shane, 26
partnership attitude at Berkshire, x, 20
passive investors, 9
Peltz, Nelson, xvii
pooling versus purchase, 58, 61, 62, 64
Pozen, Robert, 9

Price, Monroe, 79
Price Waterhouse, 58
psychology, 35, 37, 38, 39, 58
Public Company Accounting Oversight Board, 61

Qwest, 61

Reed, Brad, 25
relational investing, xv, 17-19
Repetti, James, xxi, xxv, 57, 68, 69, 72-76
Rohatyn, Felix, 68
Rudenstine, David, xxiii, 1-2, 21
Rusher, Annie, 88

Salomon Brothers, xi, xvii, 80
Sarbanes-Oxley Act, xii, 61
Scott Fetzer, xvii, 61-64, 99
second-order consequences, 12, 55
See's Candies, xx, 80, 100
short-termism, 8, 67, 68, 69, 71, 100
Simpson, Louis, xi, xxv, 28, 58, 59
social proof, 38
Sokol, David, 14
Sole, Andrew, 89
Statler Brothers, 8
Stavrou, Chris, xi, 83
Stengel, Casey, 2
stock market efficiency, xv, 31, 32, 35, 44, 46
stock splits, 29
Stout, Lynn, xxvi, 23, 34-39
strategic plans, ix, xiii, 16, 98
Supermarkets General, xi

tax policy
  foreign subsidiaries, 74
  golden parachutes, 72, 74, 75
  inequality and, 73
TIAA-CREF, xi, xxv, 7-9, 15-16
Time-Warner merger, 49, 52
Tim Hortons, xix
trivial knowledge (value of), 29-30
trust, x, xvii, 52, 60, 79, 99

volatility, 29-32

Washington Post Co., 80
Weiss, Elliott, xi, xvii, 58, 59, 77
Wesco (dividend policy), 25
Williams Act, 49
winner's curse, 38
Welch, Jack, 59
World Book, 61-62, 64
WorldCom, 61
Wyatt, Arthur, 59

Yablon, Charles, xxvi, 41, 52-56
Yankees, New York, ix, 2

CPSIA information can be obtained at www.ICGtesting.com
Printed in the USA
BVOW06s1404240416

445421BV00012B/368/P